A Choice of Scottish Verse 1560–1660

The publisher acknowledges the financial assistance of the Scottish Arts Council in the production of this volume.

A Choice of Scottish Verse
1560-1660

Selected with an Introduction

R. D. S. Jack

HODDER AND STOUGHTON
LONDON   SYDNEY   AUCKLAND   TORONTO

3

821·3

JAC

British Library Cataloguing in Publication Data

A choice of Scottish verse, 1560-1660.
   1. Scottish poetry—To 1700   2. English poetry
   —Scottish authors
   I. Jack, Ronald Dyce Sadler
   821'.3'08   PR8656

   ISBN 0-340-17559-1 Boards
   ISBN 0-340-21902-5 Paperback

Printed and bound in Great Britain for
Hodder and Stoughton Educational,
a division of Hodder and Stoughton Ltd,
Mill Road, Dunton Green, Sevenoaks, Kent,
by T. and A. Constable Ltd, Edinburgh

DEDICATION

To ignorants obdurde, quhair wilfull errour lyis,
Nor yit to curious folk, quhilks carping dois deject thee,
Nor yit to learned men, quha thinks thame onelie wyis,
But to the docile bairns of knawledge I direct thee.

James VI, The Essayes of a Prentise, 1584

CONTENTS

ACKNOWLEDGMENTS

I wish to express my gratitude to the Council of the Scottish Text Society, the Trustees of the National Library of Scotland, Edinburgh University Library, the Folger Library and the British Museum for allowing me to consult manuscripts and texts in their care. The *Review of English Studies* kindly permitted me to reprint some material from my earlier article 'The Lyrics of Alexander Montgomerie' (1969). I am also deeply indebted to Professor William Beattie, Professor C. P. Brand, Professor Gordon Donaldson, Dr Charles Haws, Mr John McGavin, Professor John MacQueen, the Revd A. M. Nicolson, Dr Richard Peterson, Mrs Mary Jane Scott and Mr James Wright for aid freely given. Finally, I am grateful to Mrs Anne McDonald and Miss Jill Strobridge for typing a difficult manuscript with such accuracy, and to my wife for her help throughout.

R. D. S. J.

INTRODUCTION

This anthology covers poetry in Scotland from the end of Mary's reign until the Restoration, a period which in England witnessed the finest works of Shakespeare, Jonson, Donne and Milton. Yet very little attention has been paid to the work of their Scottish contemporaries. Was Scottish poetry during this time so unrelievedly mediocre that silence is its wisest tribute? Had the fine example of Henryson, Dunbar, Douglas and Lindsay become only a memory? Certainly, despite the lyrics of Alexander Scott, Fethy and a few others, the later sixteenth century had seen a marked decline in the standard of Scottish vernacular verse. Of this James VI was acutely aware. In 1584, when he effectively took over the government of Scotland, he faced this problem of cultural backsliding. His own essay on literary criticism, *The Reulis and Cautelis*, represents a clear attempt to draw Scottish poetry out of its mediaeval heritage into a new renaissance liveliness, based on the precepts of the Pléiade, Puttenham, Gascoigne and others. Yet, while urging a new approach to poetry based on these earlier examples, he is also anxious to stress the individuality of this, his own Scottish Renaissance. He remarks of other critical treatises, 'that as for thame that hes written in it of late, there hes never one of thame written in our language. For albeit sindrie hes written of it in English, quhilk is lykest to our language, yit we differ from thame in sindrie reulis of Poesie, as ye will find be experience.'[1] In conception this was to be a specifically Scottish movement, led by James from the Edinburgh court as Maecenas of his 'Castalian band'.

There was, therefore, a healthy dissatisfaction with the *status quo*. On the throne was a monarch not only actively sympathetic to poetry but himself a modest practitioner in the art. His *Reulis and Cautelis*, although not stunningly original, had provided an erudite trumpet call for the new movement. Foreign poets were being invited to Edinburgh, among them

[1] *The Poems of King James VI of Scotland*, ed. J. Craigie, 2 vols., Scottish Text Society (Edinburgh, 1948), I, 67

Du Bartas, Du Bellay and Constable, so that Scotland was again establishing itself as a centre of European culture, much as it had been in the late fifteenth century. From Mary's reign James had inherited the 'maister poete', Alexander Montgomerie, and a flourishing broadsheet tradition, while the Regency had produced in the Bannatyne and Maitland Folio MSS, two valuable anthologies of earlier Scottish verse. In an attempt to build upon this inheritance he placed Montgomerie at the head of an active group of court poets, including John Stewart of Baldynneis and Queen Anne's secretary William Fowler. James's large library was open for the use of these poets, all of whom were well versed in the various rhetorical handbooks of the day. Translations and adaptations of European classics were encouraged, including James's own version of Du Bartas' *Uranie*, Fowler's reworking of Petrarch's *Trionfi* and John Stewart's expert 'abbregement' of Ariosto's *Orlando Furioso*. Even the declining interest in music had been revived by the young king. As Helena Shire remarks, 'A resumption of teaching and practice of part-music with some composition in Chapel Royal and burgh song-school alike is coeval with the fresh phase of "Castalian" poetry and song'.[1] All signs seemed set fair for the furthering of James's literary revival.

The actuality, it must be admitted, fell far short of these aspirations. Some of the reasons for this are non-literary. James's interest in a specifically Scottish renaissance died with his translation to the English court in 1603. Those of his Castalian band who went south were caught up in the English poetic movements of the day and although some, like Robert Ayton, adapted well enough, they were still conscious of writing in a medium not wholly natural to them. Meanwhile, in Edinburgh another weakness of James's renaissance was laid bare. Essentially a court movement, which had never encouraged links with the 'folk' and at times positively scorned them, it was now transplanted into foreign soil, leaving a gigantic cultural gap in the Scottish capital. Drummond of Hawthornden, one of the few Scottish poets to remain north of the border, often expresses his sense of apartness in letters to Drayton and William Alexander. James's own imperious position and temperament led to splits within the Castalian band itself. (The letters of Alexander to Drummond concerning their proposed collection of psalms chart a growing frustration as James consistently prefers his own versions to those of his collaborators.) And if personalities did not clash, awkward religious and political situations might produce undesired rifts. Thus, Montgomerie's Catholicism and Stewart's involvement in a complex legal case resulted in imprisonment for both and the withdrawing of the former's pension.

[1] Helena M. Shire, *Song, Dance and Poetry of the Court of Scotland under King James VI* (Cambridge, 1969), p. 57

The growth of Calvinistic attitudes to art has often also been advanced as a contributory reason for the overall literary mediocrity of the period. It is true that this did lead in some instances to a scorn for imagery and a love of the overexplicit approach, which produced versified sermons masquerading as poetry. On the other hand, it would be simplistic to see Calvinism as a solely negative artistic force.[1] While it clearly worked against the development of the drama in Scotland, its influence on the courtly poetry of this period is slight. In more popular verse and in the development of prose it tended to produce a reaction against excessive mannerism (which I have earlier noted) towards a more austere form of expression.

A careful study of *The Reulis and Cautelis*, however, suggests some more subtle weaknesses in James's programme for a Scottish literary revival. Most important of all, it is a 'programme' – a series of rules which, as James Craigie notes, 'tended to be purely mechanical and external'.[2] These rules were intended to help the lesser poet rather than inspire the genius, but they did encourage an unhealthy obsession with virtuoso manneristic effects in the works even of James's more talented disciples. Intelligent use of rhetoric, decorously related to meaning, characterises much of the work of Montgomerie, Stewart, Ayton and Drummond, but each occasionally practises stylistic effects as ends in themselves. Consider, for example, Stewart's extreme use of alliteration in 'Ane Literall Sonnet':

> Dull dolor dalie dois delyt destroy
> Will wantith wit waist worn with wickit wo
> Cair cankert causith confortles convoy
> Seveir sad sorow scharplie schoris so.

or of 'underwriting' in an untitled lyric:

> Ane man, ane beist, ane plant
> Is meid, is thrall, is guid,
> To serve, t'obey, to hant,
> For God, for man, for fuid.

While Stewart presumably composed these as *jeux d'esprit*, the lesser followers of the movement began to produce highsounding nothings, confident that in so doing they were in the vanguard of the new Castalian movement. This overconcern with manneristic perfection has often typified literary movements within societies of high cultural attainment, where the criticism leads the art rather than vice versa. One thinks, for example, of Italian literature, when the Accademia della Crusca with its

---

[1] See M. P. Ramsay, *Calvin and Art* (Edinburgh, 1938) p. 9
[2] *Poems of James VI*, I, xliii

heavy emphasis on metrical rules and purity of language unintentionally impeded the natural energy and originality of truly creative writers. In the highly cultured Scotland of the late sixteenth and early seventeenth centuries many of the same dangers were present.

These late 'makars' were so well equipped with the tools of rhythm, rhyming, stylistic levels and decorum that they eternally ran the risk of producing poetic buildings of grotesque complexity rather than pleasing harmony. So much was received, so much prescribed, that the only way to make an advance seemed at times to be to attempt a more daring alliterative pattern or more subtle internal rhyme than had been employed before. Nor did the danger confine itself to the realm of rhetoric. Foreign models and preconceptions of genre came into it as well. In *The Reulis and Cautelis* James shows himself to be aware of the former problem. Imitation of English, French or Italian texts is a worthy aim in itself, but if too slavishly practised, 'it will appeare, ye bot imitate, and that it cummis not of your awin Inventioun, quhilk is ane of the cheif properteis of ane poete'.[1] The many scholarly articles tracing European and English sources for Scottish works of this period have uncovered examples both of skilful adaptation and of very close translation. James, with his simplistic belief that one can make a French sonnet Scottish by turning an unknown range of French hills into the Cheviots, himself falls into the trap he critically demarcates.[2] The powerful Scottish sonnet movement in particular illustrates the great advantages of intelligent imitation but also the pitfalls of plagiarism, while among the longer verse one need only set Stewart's powerful reworking of the *Orlando Furioso* against Fowler's tedious versifying of the *Trionfi* to see what literary joys and horrors we might have missed had Scottish poets decided to ignore the literature of the Continent.

A marked development in the idea of genre is one of the major distinguishing features between the renaissance literary criticism so heartily espoused by James and its mediaeval counterpart. Mediaeval critics had a rather loose and not strictly literary definition of what constituted comedy or tragedy, romance or legend, while they relied heavily on the idea of 'voices' to distinguish between works which critics would now differentiate in terms of genre.[3] This very looseness of definition permitted adventurous tonal and thematic mixtures, which later authors, conscious of genre demarcations, either refrained from or crossed self-consciously. Ideas on comedy, tragedy, epic, lyric, sonnet, romance and so on domin-

---

[1] *Poems of James VI*, I, 78

[2] Compare James's 'The Cheviott hills doe with my state agree' and Saint Gelais' 'Voyant ces monts de veue ainsi lointaine'

[3] See P. B. Salmon, 'The Three Voices of Poetry', *Medium Aevum* (1961), vol. 30, 1-18

ated much of the critical thinking during the Scottish literary Renaissance. Again, however, this was an advance fraught with dangers for the lesser practitioner. The idea of genre, properly interpreted, might, as Alastair Fowler notes, 'enable the reader to share types of meaning economically' and advance to a new form based on the 'primary vision'.[1] John Stewart in the *Roland Furious*, while working within the genre of the romantic epic, adapts that genre with an individuality partly his own and partly derived from the wider Scottish literary tradition he inherited. The sonnet movement in Scotland profited from an awareness of the traditions of that genre in Italy, France and England. Yet in the works of James VI, William Alexander, Ayton and others one often encounters the same generic awareness less inventively deployed. Instead of the creative inspiration instinctively producing the desired literary form, one senses the reverse process, with the content being manipulated into a form *a priori* conceived by the critical mind. Much of the worst poetry in this Scottish Renaissance is that which falls dully between Professor Fowler's two categories. The 'primary vision' has been received (possibly even understood), but no advance towards a new conception has been attempted or achieved in ensuing imitations. The very clearcut forms, the analytic orderliness, the prevailing sense of stasis in all fields other than stylistics, which characterise so much Scottish poetry in our period, illustrate again the dangers inherent in a literary movement working in the shadow of an overformulated critical consciousness.

The events of Charles's reign merely accentuated these problems. With many Scottish poets based in London and a king who clearly lacked any understanding of specifically Scottish problems, Scottish literature suffered a crisis of identity from which it was only rescued by Watson and Allan Ramsay in the early eighteenth century. The 1649-60 period, when the Union of 1603 was dissolved and Scotland then conquered by Cromwell, represents a real nadir in Scottish letters. The country was, in Cromwell's own words, 'a very ruined nation', suffering under what amounted to a military occupation. Many of its leaders had suffered financial ruin, trade had reached a new low and the Scottish representatives at Westminster were merely government nominees. The ideals of James's literary renaissance were at best a memory, and the uninspired sermonising of religious poets like William Mure dominated a sad, uncertain and divided literary scene.

This has been a necessarily brief attempt to account for so much literary mediocrity at a time when the cultural and social context might have led us to expect better. Yet it is only in the last twenty years of the period that we face an almost complete dearth of good literature. Much

[1] A. D. S. Fowler, 'The Life and Death of Literary Forms' *New Literary History* (1971), vol. 2, p. 201

fine poetry was written by the 'Castalians' and their successors, as the present book will demonstrate.

As anthologies are of their own nature 'part' creations, I have chosen as far as possible to present works as a whole. The opening ballad 'Hay Trix' is, fittingly, a celebration of the downfall of Scottish Catholicism, but is balanced by the more conservative version of Richard Maitland's 'Satire upoun the Age', which laments the effect of the Reformation upon social life in the country. Robert Sempill's 'Ballat maid upoun Margret Fleming' represents the more bawdy line of verse, then so popular. All of these were composed either during the reign of Mary or during the troubled regencies prior to James VI's personal rule. The achievements of his Edinburgh reign are represented by complete texts of Montgomerie's *The Cherrie and the Slae* and Alexander Hume's *Of the Day Estivall* along with an extended extract from Stewart's *Roland Furious* and a collection of lyrics. The works of Drummond and Ayton naturally dominate the post-1603 selection, which ends with William Mure's horrified lament on the execution of Charles I and Robert Sempill's 'Elegy on Habbie Simson'. This final poem looks forward in tone and form to the eighteenth-century vernacular revival, thus providing a fitting bridge to the later movement. Among the lyrical poetry, I have specially featured the sonnet, because James saw it as the hub of his literary revival. Its popularity lasted from the early 1580s until the late 1650s. Throughout, my choice has been based on literary merit and on the desire to represent the various types of poetry popular at this time. It is hoped that such an approach will at once provide the general reader with a varied introduction to the period and the student with enough concentrated material to begin a deeper examination.

Editorially, I have tried to establish the most reliable manuscript or early printed text and used this as copy. The following concessions have been made to modern conventions. As *u*, *v* and *w* were written almost indifferently, I have introduced the modern equivalent. Likewise, when *i* is used for *j* or vice versa, I have normalised. The *ff* form has been normalised to *f* or *v*; 3 to *y* or *z* and where *y* stands for *th*, the latter form has been employed. All contractions have been expanded and capitals retained only where a modern text would have used them. Punctuation presented a more complex problem. As some of the original texts possessed little punctuation, and in others the punctuation was misleading, I have modernised the punctuation in all my selections. This modernisation, however, allows for the longer periodic structure favoured by many of the writers and in some cases for the rhetorical flow of the speaking voice. A glossary has been set beneath the text. The brief notes (pages 159-79) are intended to explain some of the more complex allusions and to indicate the more crucial textual problems.

The Cherrie and the Slae

Before any critical discussion of this poem can begin, the various textual problems should be faced. It first appeared in an unfinished and corrupt form, published by Waldegrave in 1597. Later that year, the same publisher brought out a corrected edition (here referred to as Waldegrave II), but the complete poem did not appear until 1615 under Andro Hart's imprint. This version added forty-seven stanzas to the earlier prints but unfortunately no copy of it remains. In 1636, Wreittoun published what is in all likelihood a reprint of Hart's text. The only other version which need concern us is that of Allan Ramsay in *The Evergreen* (1724). Ramsay uses Hart's version as copy, but in his usual fashion imports emendations from other texts and from his own imagination with gay abandon. Two earlier editors, James Cranstoun and H. Harvey Wood, have favoured composite texts. Cranstoun's combination of the Ramsay text with Waldegrave II is of little value. Wood more sensibly uses Waldegrave II as copy for the seventy-eight stanzas covered by that text, joining this to the extra forty-seven stanzas in Wreittoun. In this anthology I have followed the practice of the seventeenth and eighteenth centuries by employing Wreittoun as copy throughout, although as an example of the Scots language Waldegrave II is more appealing than the somewhat Anglicised Wreittoun and has been believed by many to reach greater heights of poetic skill especially in the opening May description. Whether such broad aesthetic judgments should influence an editor is another question. The facts are that Waldegrave II is an earlier and incomplete text, which I believe, with Stevenson, was probably published without the permission of the author. Wreittoun, it would appear, is a reprint of that poem as corrected and completed by the author shortly before his death. These corrections, as Helena Shire has shown in *Song, Dance and Poetry of the Court of James VI*, are quite extensive and probably influenced by Montgomerie's increasingly devout Catholicism.[1] To join Waldegrave II to Wreittoun therefore is to join two pieces of dubious compatibility in terms of the overall thematic development of the poem. I am convinced that if, following McKerrow, we wish the text which comes closest to the author's final intentions and a text which is thematically consistent, then that text must be based on Wreittoun, even although it stands at one remove from the Hart edition of 1615.

The 'persona' of the poem is encountered on a spring day in rural surroundings, watching a river plunge down from a cliff into a 'pit profound'. Cupid appears and lends him his wings. Icarus-like he soars, but wounds himself, rather than the vaguely delineated object of his search, with Cupid's arrow. He falls heavily to the earth and Cupid flies

[1] Shire, *Song, Dance and Poetry*, pp. 130-7

off, whereupon the dreamer becomes aware of the wilfulness, the ignorance and lack of reason which had caused his dilemma. It is then he sees the opposed fruits for the first time, the cherry high and almost inaccessible on the crag, the sloe easily attainable beside him on a bush. There follows a lengthy psychomachy with, broadly speaking, Courage and Hope arguing that he try for the cherry, Dread and Despair preferring the sloe. Danger's position is more complex, for although the protagonists of the cherry wish to see him as a clearcut opponent, he argues rather for the taking of further counsel. There follows the lengthy sermonising of Experience, Reason, Wit, Skill and Wisdom. Will, on the other hand, despite being responsible for the earlier disastrous assault, is unrepentant and cries for a second sudden foray. Reason eventually achieves harmony, reconciling even determined foes like Courage and Dread, Hope and Despair. Wit works out a means of climbing the cliff, but, as they progress, the fruit 'for ripnes fell'. The dreamer feels refreshed and thanks God for his love.

Even this brief synopsis emphasises the vagueness of the allegoric scheme favoured by Montgomerie. This has in its turn led critics into bitter and sometimes wrongheaded conflicts centring on the definitions of cherry and sloe. To this I shall come. Mrs Shire has given us the right lead in focusing attention initially on the differences between the earlier Waldegrave printing and the later Wreittoun version. In watching Montgomerie altering his work, we may get a clearer insight into his intentions. My own analysis of the problem pinpoints five major principles apparently followed by the author. First, he makes emendations aimed at establishing greater thematic unity. Thus during the debate between Hope and Despair, the comment in Waldegrave II that 'we can never dwell together', becomes in Wreittoun, 'we do never dwell together'. The latter reading is more consistent with the conclusion, when some harmony is achieved between the two. Similarly at Stanza 47 of the Waldegrave II text the speech 'Quhairto, suld he come heir?' is assigned to Will. In Wreittoun it is spoken by Hope. Again this is more fitting as the indictment against Danger's supposed sophistry therein contained had earlier been established as one of Hope's obsessions ('With sleikie sophismes semyng sweit' – Stanza 39). There are further subtle alterations of this sort, implying a deep involvement in the intricacies of the poem's argument and in my view rendering the possibility of non-authorial revision most unlikely.

Secondly, in Wreittoun, the opening description of the Spring day is rendered tonally more subdued by the addition of mythological parallels and asides suggestive of misery to come. The deflowering of Progne and the weeping of Apollo's paramours are introduced into the joyous May morning, while we are reminded that the cheerful labour of the bees has a serious purpose 'to stay their lives to sterve'. This rather more serious tone again anticipates the philosophical gravity of the later parts of the poem, probably not yet composed by the time of the Waldegrave print. In terms of decorum, too, we can seen why Montgomerie chose to play down the joyous rhetorical excesses of the Waldegrave opening, which, although beautiful in themselves, fit less harmoniously into the larger plan of the poem as finally conceived. Thirdly, although in Waldegrave Cupid is not directly connected with a specific amorous situation, in Wreittoun the context of his temptation is rendered even more vague. In the tenth stanza, which does not appear in Waldegrave, the concept of his 'doublenesse' is introduced, focusing on the god in one of his favoured mediaeval roles as deceiver, protagonist of illusion. Also he explicitly advises the dreamer-persona that his wings will give him 'choice . . . of a thousand things'. It seems certain that Montgomerie added this stanza to prevent readers viewing the Cupid temptation solely in terms of romance. Instead it now becomes one aspect in a wider viewing of the problem of aspiration and its human bounds. The vagueness of the associations and the allegoric apparatus up to this stage should have given adequate warning, but Montgomerie – rightly as it turned out – feared that many would make the simplistic Cupid = love equation without further thought.

Fourthly, as befits a makar, Montgomerie quite frequently alters particular words as well as the broader patterns of his rhetoric. He omits ineffective repetitions, adds puns and regularly replaces adjectives or adverbs of physical description with more abstract, allusive ones (for example, Waldegrave II has 'As to the sey it [the river] *swiftlie* slaid', but Wreittoun has *softly*). This last class of alterations also adds force to the theory of a conscious philosophic deepening of the poem in revision. The fifth class of alterations, in many ways the most important, confirms this last point. The poet's major insertion within the scope of the Walde-grave text (Stanzas 58-66 in this anthology) introduces the Thomist/Scotist debate between Reason and Will. Montgomerie, who in the later years of his life indicated his desire to become a friar, would obviously be attracted to one of the major patristic debates. While the nature of the poem – and probably his own inclinations – prevented him from entering into the intricacies of this argument, he clearly sides with Aquinas in supporting the primacy of Reason. More generally, the greatest distinguishing feature between Waldegrave and Wreittoun is the development of the psychomachy in the latter. The extended parts played by such as Reason, Wit and Wisdom, the equation of Youth and desire, the emphasising of the Augustinian pattern of temptation in ignorance then experience – all these alterations and additions are consistent with the theory of a poet reworking an earlier (probably incomplete) poem in terms of his own growing religious enthusiasm. The overall result, if considered in relation to late mediaeval poetic practice, is by no means unpleasing.

Earlier comment on the poem, however, reminds one of the critical fate of the *Kingis Quair*. In each case there is a refusal to see that an initially romantic poem may easily widen into a probing of the philosophic problems there raised in embryo. Cranstoun unconsciously echoes Skeat's reception of the *Quair* when he complains about Montgomerie's allegory, that 'the earlier portion of the poem (ll.1-392) is a love piece, while the remainder partakes of the nature of a moral poem'.[1] He would have done well to take more careful note of the seventeenth-century commentator Dempster, who suggested that the poem foreshadowed an opposition both between highborn lady and humble mistress and between Vice and Virtue. Although the latter contrast is rather too stark to mirror the changing subtleties of the debate, Dempster is anticipating Helena Shire's judgment, when she calls it a 'maniefalde allegorie', capable of interpretation on different levels. (With this I agree.) There is the physical level on which the fruits are real, the romantic level of distant and accessible loves, the broad tropological level covering oppositions like those between aspiration and humble contentment, possibly the political level stressed by Mrs Shire, with the cherry representing the crown of Britain dangling before James VI, and the religious level suggesting opposition between Catholicism (cherry) and Protestantism (sloe). Allegorical and anagogical interpretations might further lead us to identify the cherry tree with acceptance of Christ, or with the grace which leads to salvation. This final equation is first suggested by the presence of the river, itself a symbol for grace, which the dreamer-persona has to cross before achieving his goal. It also explains the undramatic ease with which the fruit is finally obtained. As the cherry falls of its own accord, we may remember that, according to Aquinas, grace was ready for man at all times. Only his blindness (now cured by the psychomachy) prevents this gift from being given to him. So *The Cherrie and the Slae* effectively mirrors the theological truth that impossible quests are rendered easy by turning to God and accepting the gift of his grace.

But are we not reading too much into the poem? The work is essentially written in the mediaeval tradition, when interpretation on many levels was encouraged. It is also – especially in the Wreittoun text – self-consciously open-ended in the imagery and vocabulary it employs. That is, much as in the court comedies of Lyly, the author seems intentionally to be maintaining in his allegory not a vagueness but an associative open-

[1] *Poems of Alexander Montgomerie*, ed. James Cranstoun, Scottish Text Society (Edinburgh, 1887), p. xxix

ness which tempts the reader into redefining the symbolic values of cherry and sloe as the poem progresses. The reader begins to create as well as to receive. Like the dreamer he begins to indulge in a personal psycho-machy, not wholly controlled by the poem, and reflected in the pre-dominant symbolic values he assigns to cherry and sloe.

The relationship of the poem to James's Renaissance is an intriguing one. The clever rhetorical effects, complex rhyming stanza and musical setting must have pleased James in his Maecenas role, for he uses examples from the poem in *The Reulis and Cautelis*. The mingling of various genres – dream vision, *chanson d'aventure*. *débat* – is also in the tradition of that prescriptive treatise. Most obviously, the many echoes from other works, which fleetingly reach the surface of the poem but in no way destroy its individuality, form a perfect working model for the king's critical discussion of Imitation and Invention. Yet the 'maister poete' was never as faithful a disciple as other members of the Castalian band, having after all established his reputation prior to its creation. One might justi-fiably deduce that the patristic base to the poem, the veiled dissatisfaction with the monarch's religious policies and the essentially mediaeval form of the work would cause the king some concern as he strove to bring Scotland into its literary Renaissance and out of its Catholic past.

Roland Furious

Stewart of Baldynneis, the author of *Roland Furious*, differed from Montgomerie in being a member of the Castalian band with no earlier reputation. In the introduction to his poems he addresses James as follows: 'Sir, haifing red your majesteis maist prudent precepts in the devyn art of poesie, I haif assayit my sempill spreit to becum your hienes scholler'.[1] An awareness of *The Reulis and Cautelis* is evident throughout his work, at times constricting a vivid imagination, poetically far superior to the king's. His 'abbregement' of Ariosto's *Orlando Furioso* was undertaken as part of James's plan for rendering great European masterpieces into Scots, while his other long work, *Ane Schersing out of trew Felicitie*, intro-duces sycophantic praise of that monarch at the slightest excuse and sometimes with incongruously comic effect.

Roland Furious, rightly called by M. P. McDiarmid, 'the most brilliant and energetic poem of the brief Scots Renaissance',[2] isolates two major strands from the complex story of Ariosto's poem. These concern the

[1] *Poems of John Stewart of Baldynneis*, ed. T. Crockett, 2 vols., Scottish Text Society (Edinburgh, 1913) II, 3

[2] M. P. McDiarmid, 'Notes on the Poems of John Stewart of Baldynneis', *Review of English Studies* (1948), vol. 24, p. 17

careers of Orlando and Angelica, culminating with the former's madness and the latter's marriage to Medoro. What is immediately noticeable is Stewart's determination, within the frame of the work as newly defined, to highlight parallels and contrasts; to impose a neat pattern upon an original, which he considered at times 'a tedius and prolixit history'. At the simplest level this might imply a series of parallel laments, with Sacripanto's in Canto II being followed by Angelica's in Canto III and Orlando's in Canto IV. Themes which are unobtrusively worked into the Italian poem are much more obsessionally pursued by Stewart. Ariosto clearly intended the *Furioso* at one level to be a study of different types of love. Stewart, using Angelica as a focus, examines this problem much more explicitly. One suitor follows another almost like a series of mediaeval *exempla*. There is the comic wooing of Sacripanto, falling from heights of *hubris* to depths of shame, as he is unhorsed before his lady by the female knight Bradamante. This contrasts with the tragic passion of Rinaldo, doomed to futility by the fates. The impotent lustfulness of the hermit is then set against Ruggiero's high ideals, only for the latter to fall victim to lust himself. Finally the high chivalric love of Orlando is rejected while the more modest affection of Medoro pleases Angelica.

In all this we feel the presence of an orderly analytic intellect at work, constantly intent on restructuring. Numerous parallels between Orlando and Angelica implicitly present in the Italian are explicitly stressed in the Scottish 'abbregement'. Both fall through sins against God, one by deserting the Christian cause, the other through pride. One conquers love after a long period of subjugation, the other is entrapped by love after disdaining it. Yet by these different paths they find inner harmony, because one adds passion to her overpowering intellect, the other finds reason where earlier the madness of passion had reigned.

Stewart is always striving to arrange his material in orderly fashion. Thus the idea of chastity and the conflict between love and honour are also drawn in as thematic leitmotives. In short, although he shares Ariosto's attitude to most matters, he prefers explicitness to implicitness, the balance of symbolic instances to the lights and shadows of narrative, and a rigid scheme to the more natural but somewhat amorphous structure of the *Furioso*. Timothy Nelson, in his stimulating article 'John Stewart of Baldynneis and *Orlando Furioso*', comes to a similar conclusion, when he comments: 'Ariosto's habit is to mingle genres, to cross one with another, to stand back and view each ironically in the light of the rest. But Stewart's irresistible urge is to put everything back in its pigeon-hole.'[1] This approach arises from the genre consciousness and the simplistic

---

[1] Timothy Nelson, 'John Stewart of Baldynneis and *Orlando Furioso*', *Studies in Scottish Literature* (1968), vol. 6, p. 106

literary assumptions which characterised so much of the thinking among James's Castalian band. Stewart does create something new and valuable from his model, but this creation is recognisably based on 'the conscious knowledge of the primary vision'. The use of rhetoric is equally controlled by Stewart's understanding of genre. As Nelson puts it: 'Stewart infuses a heightened seriousness into Sacripanto's speech mainly because it belongs to a genre – the love-complaint – which is inseparably associated in his mind with a mood of dignified pathos'.[2] Here again *The Reulis and Cautelis* with their detailed laws for decorum were probably uppermost in the writer's mind. Stewart's claim to be the king's apprentice was no mere literary compliment. Unfortunately, much that seems rather mechanical in the work of this talented craftsman may plausibly be attributed to his strict critical allegiance.

Rhetorically, too, the *Roland Furious* presents a variety of forms which must have delighted James. Stewart's more extreme experiments are placed in suitable contexts – passionate laments, pastoral descriptions, highpoints of dramatic conflict. Thus, when the device of 'ryming ryme' is employed in imitation of the *grands rhétoriqueurs*, it is used to underline the poignancy of Sacripanto's lament on his unsuccessful wooing:

> Dispair consums me confortles in cair,
> Cair dois ourcum my corps with cair confound,
> Confound I am, my mychtis may na mair,
> Mair yit I may, my luif dois mair abound,
> Abounding luife of all my greife is ground,
> Ground find I non, quhair onnie grace dois grow.

And when the Italianate technique of underwriting is used, it is generally to mark the climax of some momentous action, as when Stewart is describing Roland's martial might in Canto I or, more powerfully, the height of his madness in Canto XI:

> He raifs, he rugs, he bruisis, breaks and ryfs
> With hands, with feit, with nails, and teith alway;
> He byts, he stricks, he tumbls, he turns, he stryfs,
> He glaiks, he gaips, he girns, he glours, he dryfs
> Throw moss, and montane, forrest, firth, and plaine,
> The birds, the beists, the bayes, the men and wyfs.

In all this, as in his use of initial repetition, lists, question series and lengthy homeric similes, there is the self-consciousness of the makar. One gets

---

[2] *Ibid.* p. 108

used to the narrative breaking off for a lyrical setpiece and to the gradual increase in rhetorical virtuosity, as the action reaches its climax. The overall effect is very pleasing, although the modern reader does have to take into account the critical background against which the poet was writing and modify his tastes accordingly.

The problems of Imitation and Invention raised by the 'abbregement' are many and complex. It is clear that, at points, Stewart has used Desportes' *Roland Furieux* and *Angélique* as intermediary sources. This is most obviously so in the opening Canto and for the climax scenes celebrating Angelica's love and Orlando's madness. Yet Desportes' Ariostan adaptations do not cover nearly as much ground as does Stewart. Quite frequently in the remaining portions of Stewart's *Roland* he has used another French text, Jean Martin's prose version of 1543, then available in Scotland. As Martin's translation sets out to be a very literal one, significant departures from the Italian original are few and far between. When they do occur, however, Stewart tends to follow Martin:

> Dando già il sole *alla sorella* loco   (Ariosto)
> Donnant lieu *à sa soeur Phebe*   (Martin)
> *Till his pale sister Phebe* giffing place   (Stewart)

One also notes that in instances where the French text's very literalness leads it into realms of ambiguity, this ambiguity is reflected by Stewart, or the relevant passage is merely omitted.

The strongest evidence stems from word-forms. Time and again Stewart chooses a translation which comes suspiciously close to the French word favoured by Martin. One of the most striking examples of this occurs in Canto III, during the battle between Sacripanto and Rinaldo. The fear of Angelica is expressed in the Italian as follows:

> Quando vide *la timida donzella*
> Dal fiero colpo uscir tanta ruina,
> Per gran timor cangio la faccia bella.

This becomes in the prose of Martin, 'Quand *la pucelle craintive* veit du fier coup sortir si grand ruyne, par grand crainte changea sa belle face'. Stewart, although generally following a rather free translation procedure, here echoes the French description of Angelica very closely indeed:

> Quhilk quhan *the craintive pucelle* haid espyit,
> With wo all vext hir hands began to wring,
> And doutfull dreid hir beutie brycht updryit.

Examples of this sort could easily be multiplied. On the whole, I believe (with M. P. McDiarmid) that the poet read Ariosto in the original, but would maintain that both Desportes and Martin were frequently used as intermediary texts. This very professional approach to the problems of translation was generally shared by the Castalians, as William Fowler's introduction to his *Triumphs* confirms. There he claims not only to have studied Petrarch's Italian original but also the many 'Frenche and Inglish traductionis' currently available to him. The approaches are similar, although Stewart's efforts were more happily translated into art.

In direct contrast to *The Cherrie and the Slae*, the textual problems posed by *Roland Furious* are slight. The poem exists in a single MS, which also contains the rest of Stewart's known work. This book, which is among the manuscript holdings of the National Library of Scotland, has 160 leaves and measures $10\frac{3}{8}'' \times 7\frac{1}{2}''$. It has a handsome sixteenth-century binding in morocco, gold-tooled and stamped on both sides with the initials I R (Iacobus Rex) and a crown. The edge of the boards is gilt. The poetry is written in a regular, easily decipherable, semi-Italian hand, with the text set within an inner square of double red lines. The 'apprentice' apparently gave this manuscript as a gift to his mentor-monarch, and it is recorded that James VI valued it highly. This is scarcely surprising. It is an outstandingly beautiful manuscript and contains verse composed in obedience to James's own 'precepts in the devyn art of poesie'. The monarch's insatiable ego could scarcely fail to be boosted by such a gift.

The Lyric and the Sonnet

After 1603, Scottish poetry became more Anglicised. In terms of general comparative patterns, Scottish poets began to look to Italian and English models, where earlier they might have favoured the mediaeval Scottish makars and the French. Middle Scots became less and less favoured as a medium by the court poets, who preferred to attempt mastery of the English tongue. In a situation like this it is inevitable that many false artistic roads were embarked upon and rejected. I may therefore be forgiven if I simplify the picture by highlighting the leaders of the three most successful lyrical movements espoused by Scotsmen in the Jacobean and Caroline eras.

At the Edinburgh court prior to 1603 the lead was given by Montgomerie. In his lyrical verse the 'maister poete' drew from three distinct traditions. There was first the influence of the French *rhétoriqueurs*, and Molinet in particular. The French writer had, for example, advocated a verse form with three longer lines and one short 'pour amoureuses complaintes et autres doléances'. Montgomerie obeys this in the plaintive 'Example for his Lady':

> Now, lovesome lady, let us leir
> Example of these ladyis heir;
> Sen Daphne boght his love so deir,
> Hir fortun suld effray you.

Molinet's *vers enchayenné*, where 'la fin d'un mètre est pareil en voix au commencement de l'autre', is adapted successfully (in Sonnet 43 in the Cranstoun Scottish Text Society edition):

> I trow your love by loving so unsene;
> Unsene siklyk I languish for your love:
> Your love is comely, constant, chaste and clene.

The unobtrusive use of the echoing device here, especially when contrasted with Stewart's more theatrical use of the technique, highlights a major feature of Montgomerie's approach. While working within the rhetorical tradition, he regularly modifies it in ways which might be called popular. He simplifies stanza forms and rhetorical devices; he refuses to see style as an end in itself and regularly uses courtly forms as a vehicle for sincerity.

So, when it is suggested that his extensive use of proverbs in both lyrics and *The Cherrie and the Slae* indicates popular influence, one ought to counter with the comment that proverbs were also favoured by the *rhétoriqueurs*, especially as a means of clinching a stanza. Molinet writes: 'Autres vers de sept sillabes et de sept lignes sont trouvez en plusieurs euvres, dont la derraine ligne chiet en commun proverbe'. Montgomerie was doubtless attracted to popular modes. He was not, after all, a nobleman. He came to Edinburgh from rural Ayrshire, where hierarchical distinctions were not so clear as in the city. He appears from his verse to have enjoyed mixing with ordinary men and his poetry breathes a democratic spirit lacking in that of most Castalians. Yet he was also a court poet valued by the King for that reason, and his democracy for the most part expresses itself through emphases within the courtly conventions, rather than transgressions of their rules.

This process of simplification is aided by the second flourishing court tradition from which Montgomerie drew inspiration – that of music. The revival of interest in music at the court of James VI has been thoroughly treated by Mrs Shire. Montgomerie, who regularly set his lyrics to the tunes of his day, is led to simplify his metres, to shorten line lengths and compose in more regular stanza forms than had, say, a pure rhetorician like Dunbar. He especially favours lilting rhythms with short/long line alternations and dominant rhymes, a combination which inevitably looks back to Alexander Scott and forward to Burns. Even his versions of the psalms are predominantly set in these light, lyrical metres:

Blest is the man,
Yea, happie than,
By grace that can
Eschew ill counsell and the godles gates;
And walkes not in
The way of sin,
Nor doth begin
To sit with mockers in the scornfull sates.

Each of these alterations points away from professional virtuosity towards a more popular type of verse. Just as in the case of the proverbs, however, the motivations are not primarily popular ones. The demands of music rather than the folk are correctly to be seen as the simplifying agents, while the skills of the rhetorician are never absent.

A study of the third tradition from which Montgomerie drew produces very similar conclusions. One is conscious of occasional echoes from Ovid, Tibullus and other classical writers. Yet they are consciously underplayed and do not become the centre of the argument as in the later lyrics of Alexander Craig. When Craig handles a classical analogy he tends to imitate the classical style and to adopt an intentionally erudite tone (except in the sonnets to Kala). When Montgomerie chooses to remind us of the legend of Echo and Narcissus, he does so with the light lyricism of the musical tradition and focuses attention on the memorable refrain:

To the, Echo, and thou to me agane.

The tripping metre and episodic techniques used in 'Before the Greeks durst enterpryse' likewise transform the Greek consultations of the oracle at Delphos into a near-ballad. It is this mixture which constitutes the major charm and the originality of Montgomerie's verse. Molinet's rhetorical demands may influence one line, classical education the next, and musical considerations the third. Montgomerie moves from one mode to another, taking the best qualities from each and using the respective characteristics of each tradition for skilful contrasts and counterpointing. All three are synthesized by his simpler, democratic vision of life – a non-courtly mind, which expresses itself naturally (at times pungently) in Middle Scots:

I, Richie, Jane, and George are lyk to dee;
Four crabbit crippilis crackand in our crouch.
Sen I am trensh-man for the other thrie,
Let drunken Pancrage drink to me in Dutch.

His tragedy is that he is a transition poet for a movement which postponed its inauguration for over a hundred years and then had a much inferior, if more committed, herald in Allan Ramsay.

The two major lyricists of the post-1603 period are William Drummond of Hawthornden and Sir Robert Ayton. Essentially they had aligned themselves with opposed sides in the English literary controversy of their day. Drummond, in his friendship with Drayton and his professed preference for the Spenserean approach to art, stood for the more conservative, decorative type of lyric. Ayton, whose close friendship with Ionson and 'the witts of his time' is mentioned by Aubrey, belonged to the new line of 'wit' in poetry. From this point of view it must be stressed that, although an admirer of Donne, his verse seldom achieves that poet's adventurousness of image. While in Donne tenor and vehicle of the metaphors employed create a new concept by powerful imaginative synthesis, Ayton plays cleverly with parallels, yet never forces a fusion:

> Lov's like a game at Irish where the dye
> Of maids affection doth by fortune fly,
> Which, when you thinke you certaine of the same,
> Proves but att best a doubtfull aftergame.

His intellect like Donne's is ever-active, yet when he seizes upon a time-worn conceit he does not wholly transmute it, but confines himself to adding a clever final quirk, as in 'Upone a Gentlewoman that painted':

> What thinke you this a prodigie? Its none,
> The painter and the picture were both one.

Like Donne, too, he enjoys creating a complex logical pattern within the poem, based usually on a conceit of some complexity. In advancing this, he employs paradox, wordplay, epigram and antithesis, again in metaphysical fashion. Yet, unlike Donne, he refuses to give the argument free rein, breaking down the neat formal structure with the energy of imaginative thought. Enjambments, irregular stanzas and the more daring imaginative leaps are missing in the somewhat clinical, though highly polished lyrics of Ayton.

There are two ways to view this evidence. One could with some justification draw him into the English tradition and link him with the wit of later Caroline lyricists such as Suckling. Yet, to look behind rather than before, one might equally argue that many recognisably Castalian traits can be detected in Ayton's work. There is this very interest in formal perfection, the clever adaptation of the sonnet form in particular to the development of logical argument (as counselled in *The Reulis and Cautelis*), the love of orderliness on all levels and the unswerving critical obedience to the rules of decorum. Indeed, in many ways Ayton's verse is the natural successor to James's own, although Ayton is endowed with a more fertile imagination and is more heavily committed to the use of metaphor and simile as prime poetic devices. Also, there is the sense of apartness, perhaps accentuated by the influence of the English court. The Scots poet seems to be working from outside rather than being part of the mainstream of creative metaphysical verse. He starts from a critical awareness of genre and the demands of rhetoric rather than redefining these by completely immersing himself in the requirements of his own art.

Montgomerie, without departing from courtly precedent, managed to create for himself a unique and personal lyrical voice. It is doubtful whether Ayton managed to do the same, although technically his lyrical verse, in whatever genre, is among the finest produced by Scotsmen in this period. The third major figure, Drummond of Hawthornden, might initially seem to share this weakness. After all, few poets can claim to have assimilated into their poetry so many foreign voices. Desportes, Passerat, Ronsard, Bertaut, Petrarch, Tasso, Marino, Guarini, Boscan, Garcilaso, Sidney, Fowler, Alexander – the list is endless. Like Hugh MacDiarmid, the leader of the modern Scottish makars, he welcomed all earlier and contemporary literature as material for his poetic inspiration. Yet through all this Drummond, no less than MacDiarmid, has a profoundly original viewpoint and voice. Thematically, he is obsessed with the ideas of death, loneliness, mutability and an instinctive hatred of wordly values. These are explicitly treated in his prose work *Ane Cypresse Grove*. In *The Scottish Sonnet* and *Renaissance Poetry*, I tried to show that his lyrical sequence *The Flowres of Sion*, while yielding many foreign models for the comparative critic, was unified by a conscious attempt to combat these fears with the promises held out by the Christian religion.[1] Thematic interests of this sort largely determine Drummond's choice of sources and his manner of adapting them. Thus, the work of a minor poet may be treated, when he is composing on a topic dear to Drummond's heart:

> Questo mondo e una caccia, e cacciatrice
> La Morte vincitrice
> I veltri suoi rapaci
> Sono cure mordaci
> E morbi, e mal, da cui cacciati siamo,
> E se talhor fuggiamo,
> Vecchiezza sua compagna,
> Ci prende ne la regna
>
> (Belli)

[1] Edinburgh University Ph.D. Thesis, 1968

This world a Hunting is,
The pray poore Man, the Nimrod fierce is Death,
His speedie Grei-hounds are,
Lust, sicknesse, Envie, Care,
Strife that neere falles amisse,
With all those ills which haunt us while wee breath.
Now, if, (by chance) wee flie
Of these the eager Chase,
Old Age with stealing Pace,
Castes up his Nets and there wee panting die.

(Drummond)

The poem by Valerio Belli unites all four of Drummond's major thematic obsessions and this was almost certainly the cause of the Scottish poet's interest in it.

Bembo, of course, was a much more renowned figure than Belli, yet Drummond very seldom turned to his verse for inspiration. The exception made in the case of 'Lieta è chiusa contrada', by no means an outstanding poem in Bembo's canon, is probably due to its treating the subject of loneliness and the value of rural retreats, a theme which recurs frequently in Drummond's writings. Yet it is noticeable that when Bembo in the second quatrain introduces quasi-religious sentiments, somewhat at odds with Drummond's known position, the Scottish poet omits the lines and instead develops the theme of contentment. For Bembo the grave mystically cures all ills. Drummond, in 'Deare wood you sweet solitare place', prefers more realistically to see it as a retreat where problems may be reassessed in a spirit of restfulness, before being faced again. In so doing, he once more imposes personal vision upon derivative subject matter.

This personal vision is not the only source of Drummond's originality. From this point of view the medium is every bit as important as the message. Many of the major stylistic features stressed so perceptively by Ruth Wallerstein[1] – the more static and Latinate style, the clearcut rhetorical approach, the parenthetic moralisations – had all been characteristics of earlier Castalian writing. Like Montgomerie, Drummond avoided imitating the virtuoso extremes of this school, contributing his own delicate use of metaphor, his unmistakable tonal norm of wistful melancholy and a use of alliteration and assonance which is as gentle and subtle as James's is aggressive and direct:

[1] Ruth Wallerstein, 'The Style of Drummond of Hawthornden in its relation to his translations', *PMLA* (1933), vol. 48, pp. 1089-1107

Sound hoarse sad lute, true witnesse of my woe,
And strive no more to ease selfe-chosen paine
With soule-enchanting sounds, your accents straine
Unto these teares uncessantly which flow.

Although Montgomerie and Drummond, respective 'maister poetes' of
the pre- and post-1603 periods, have many differences, their mingling
of imitation with originality and their playing down of prevalent literary
excesses bring them on to common ground.

Finally, the collection of sonnets assembled in this volume (pages 139-
58) permits the student to trace the development of that genre throughout
the period of its greatest popularity. In the early period, when French
and earlier Scottish sources predominate, there are James's own formal
love sonnets to Anne of Denmark, the Ronsardian adaptations of Mont-
gomerie, and Stewart's many-sided viewing of the passion from worship
to bawdry. The major love sequences, by way of contrast, are Italianate
in origin. Fowler's *Tarantula*, following a clearcut narrative line, traces
also a Ficinian progression from physical lust to a spiritual acceptance
of God. Alexander in *Aurora* prefers a more philosophical approach,
stressing the various oppositions inherent in the passion. He finally finds
comfort by stressing the values of synthesis, aspiration and an observation
of Nature's greater constancy. By so doing he transcends love and can
advance to higher topics. David Murray's *Caelia* is at once an amatory
sequence and, more subtly, a protest against the vagaries of fate, as
mirrored in the untimely death of his friend Henry, Prince of Wales.
Perhaps more immediately striking, however, is Alexander Craig's
Amorose Songes in which he hymns eight mistresses, each representing a
different aspect of love from highest ideals to lowest whoredom. When
one adds to all this the mystical sonnets of William Mure and a wide
variety of single efforts in the genre, it can be seen that the better-known
works of Ayton and Drummond were not created in a cultural vacuum,
but were the crowning point of a very active movement. Over 800
Scottish sonnets of this period have been preserved, forming not the
least worthy monument for James's literary Renaissance.

R. D. S. Jack

Edinburgh
May 1975

Anonymous

Hay Trix, Tryme go Trix

1   The Paip, that pagane full of pride
    He hes us blindit lang,
    For quhair the blind the blind dois gyde,
    Na wonder thay ga wrang:
    Like prince and king he led the ring
    Of all iniquitie,
    Hay trix, tryme go trix, under the grene (wode tree).

2   Bot his abhominatioun
    The Lord hes brocht to licht;
    His popische pride and thrinfald crowne
    Almaist hes loist thair micht;
    His plak pardounis ar bot lardounis
    Of new found vanitie,
    Hay trix, tryme go trix, under the grene wode tree.

3   His Cardinallis hes caus to murne,
    His Bischoppis borne aback:
    His Abbottis gat ane uncouth turne
    Quhen schavelingis went to sack.
    With burges wyfis thay led thair lyfis
    And fure better nor we,
    Hay trix, tryme go trix, under the grene wode tree.

4   His Carmelites and Jacobinis,
    His Dominiks had greit do,
    His Cordeleiris and Augustinis,
    Sanct Frances ordour to.
    Thay sillie freiris, mony yeiris,
    With babling blerit our e,
    Hay trix, tryme go trix, under the grene wode tree.

thrinfald triple   *plak* farthing   *lardounis* shams (?)   *turne* fright
schavelingis ecclesiastics   *fure* fared
had greit do made a great song and dance about   *blerit* blinded

5   The Sisteris gray, before this day,
    Did crune within their cloister.
    Thay feit ane freir, thair keyis to beir,
    The feind ressave the foster,
    Syne in the mirk sa weill culd wirk
    And kittill thame wantounlie,
    Hay trix, tryme go trix, under the grene wode tree.

6   The blind Bischop, he culd not preiche
    For playing with the lassis:
    The syllie Freir behuffit to fleiche
    For almous that he assis:
    The Curat, his Creid he culd nocht reid,
    Schame fall the cumpanie,
    Hay trix, tryme go trix, under the grene wode tree.

7   The Bischop wald nocht wed ane wife,
    The Abbote not persew ane,
    Thankand it was ane lustie life
    Ilk day to have ane new ane,
    In everie place ane uncouth face
    His lust to satisfie,
    Hay trix, tryme go trix, under the grene wode tree.

8   The Persoun wald nocht have ane hure
    Bot twa, and thay war bony:
    The Vicar (thocht that he was pure)
    Behuiffit to have als mony:
    The Parris Preist, that brutall beist,
    He polit thame privelie,
    Hay trix, tryme go trix, under the grene wode tree.

9   Of Scotlandwell the Freiris of Faill,
    The lymmerie lang hes lestit:
    The Monkis of Melros maid gude kaill
    On Frydayis quhen thay fastit:
    The sillie Nunnis caist up thair bunnis
    And heisit thair hippis on hie,
    Hay trix, tryme go trix, under the grene wode tree.

---

feit hired   *feind* devil   *foster* child   *kittill* tickle
behuffit needed   *fleiche* flatter   *assis* asks   *pure* poor   *polit* fleeced
lymmerie villainy   *kaill* broth   *bunnis* bums   *heisit* raised

10   Of lait I saw thir lymmaris stand
       Like mad men at mischeif;
       Thinking to get the upper hand
       Thay luke efter releif,
       Bot all in vaine, go tell thame plaine,
       That day will never be,
       Hay trix, tryme go trix, under the grene wode tree.

11   O Jesus, gif thay thocht greit glie
       To see Goddis word downe smorit,
       The Congregatioun made to flie,
       Hypocresie restorit
       With Messis sung and bellis rung
       To thair idolatrie,
       Marie God thank you, we sall gar brank you,
       Befoir that time trewlie.

thir lymmaris those rascals   *smorit* smothered
brank punish with iron bridle and gag

Sir Richard Maitland

Satire on the Age

1   Quhair is the blythnes that hes bein
Bayth in burgh and landwart sein,
Amang lordis and ladyis schein
Daunsing, singing, game and play?
Bot now I wait nocht quhat thai mein,
All mirrines is worne away.

2   For now I heir na wourde of yule
In kirk, on cassay nor in scule,
Lordis lattis thair kitchings cule
And draws thame to the abbay
And scant hes ane to keip thair mule,
All houshaldaris is worne away.

3   I saw no gysaris all this yeir
Bot kirkmen cled lyk men of weir,
That never cummis in the queir;
Lyk ruffyanis is thair array,
To preiche and teiche that will nocht leir,
The kirk gudis thai waist away.

4   Kirkmen affoir war gude of lyf,
Preichit, teichit and stanchit stryf,
Thai feirit nother swerd nor knyf;
For luif of god the suyth to say,
All honorit thame bayth man and wyf,
Devotioun was nocht away.

5   Our faderis wyse was and discreit,
Thay had bayth honor, men and meit,
With luif thai did thair tennents treit
And had aneuche in poiss to lay,
Thay wantit nother malt nor quheit
And mirriness was nocht away.

landwart country	*schein* beautiful	*wait* know	*cassay* pavement
scant scarcely	*mule* concubine	*gysaris* mummers	*queir* choir
leir learn	*suyth* truth	*poiss* hoard	

6 And we hald nother yule nor pace
  But seik our meit from place to place,
  And we have nother luk nor grace,
  We gar our landis doubill pay,
  Our tennentis cryis alace, alace,
  That reuth and petie is away.

7 Now we have mair it is weill kend
  Nor our foirbearis had to spend,
  Bot far less at the yeiris end
  And never hes ane mirrie day,
  God will na rychess to us send
  Sa lang as honour is away.

8 We waist far mar now lyk vane fulis,
  We and our page to turss our mulis,
  Nor thai did than that held grit yulis,
  Off meit and drink said never nay;
  Thay had lang formes quhair we have stulis
  And mirrines was nocht away.

9 Off our wanthrift sum wytis playis
  And sum their wantoun vane arrayis,
  Sum the wyt on thair wyffis layis,
  That in the court wald gang so gay,
  And caris nocht quha the merchant payis
  Quhill pairt of land be put away.

10 The kirkmen keipis na professioun,
  The temporale men committis oppressioun,
  Puttand the pure from thair possessioun;
  Na kynd of feir of god have thai,
  Thai cummar bayth the court and sessioun
  And chassis cheritie away.

11 Quhen ane of thame sustenis wrang
  We cry for justice heid and hang,
  Bot quhen our nychtbor we ourgang
  We laubor justice to delay;
  Effectioun blindis us sa lang,
  All equitie is put away.

pace Easter *turss* carry off *wanthrift* lack of thriving
cummar burden *ourgang* trick

12   To mak actis we have sum feill,
        God wait gif that we keip thame weill;
        We cum to bar with jak of steill
        As we wald bost the juge and fray;
        Off sic justice I have na skeill,
        Quhair rewle and ordour is away.

13   Our lawis are lichtleit for abusioun,
        Sumtyme is clokit with collusioun,
        Quhilk causis of blude the greit effusioun
        For na man sparis now to slay.
        Quhat bringis cuntreis to confusioun
        Bot quhair that justice is away?

14   Quhair is the wyt quha can schaw us?
        Quha bot our nobillis that suld knaw us
        And till honorabill deidis draw us?
        Lat never commoun weill decay
        Or ellis sum mischeif will faw us
        And nobilnes we put away.

15   Put our awin lawis to executioun!
        Apone trespassouris mak punitioun!
        To cruell folk seik na remissioun!
        For peax and justice lat us pray,
        In dreid sum strange new institutioun
        Cum and our custome put away.

16   Amend your lyveis ane and all,
        And be war of ane suddane fall,
        And pray to god that maid us all,
        To send us joy that lestis ay,
        And let us nocht to syn be thrall,
        Bot put all vyce and wrang away.

feill knowledge   *jak* jacket   *bost* threaten
skeill skill   *lichtleit* condemned   *faw* befall

Aganis the Theivis of Liddisdaill

1   Off Liddisdaill the commoun thevis
     Sa peirtlie stelis now and revis,
     That nane can keip hors, nolt nor scheip,
     Nor yit dar sleip for thair mischevis.

2   Thai planelie throw the cuntrey rydis,
     I trow the mekle deill thame gydis,
     Quhair thai on sett, ay in thai gett,
     Thair is na yet nor dure thame bydis.

3   Thai leif rycht nocht quhair eir thai ga,
     Thair can na thing be hid thame fra,
     For giff men wald thair housis hald,
     Than wax thai bald, to burne and sla.

4   Thai have neir hand hirreit haill
     Ettrik forrest and Lauderdaill;
     Now ar thai gane in Lowthiane
     And sparis nane, that thai will waill.

5   Thai landis ar with stouthe sa socht
     To extreme povertie ar brocht
     Thai wickit schrewis, hes laid the plewis
     That nane or few is that ar left ocht.

6   Be commoun taking of blak maile,
     Thai that had flesche, gud breid and aile
     Now ar sa wrakit, maid pure and nakit,
     Fane to be stakit with watir caile.

7   Thai thevis that stelis and tursis hame,
     Ilkane of thame hes ane to name –
     Will of the Lais, Hab of the Schais –
     To mak bair wais thai think na schame.

peirtlie boldly	*revis* thieves	*nolt* cattle	*deill* devil
on sett attack	*yet* gate	*bydis* withstands	*hirreit* plundered
waill choose	*stouthe* theft	*socht* attacked	*plewis* ploughs
wrakit ruined	*stakit* supported	*watir caile* vegetable broth	
tursis carries	*to name* nickname	*mak bair wais* scorch the land	

8   Thai spulye pure men of thair pakis,
          Thai leif thame nocht on bed nor bakis,
          Baythe hen and cok, with reill and rok,
          The lairdis Jok all with him takis.

9   Thai leif not spindle, spune nor speit,
          Bed boustar, blancat, sark nor scheit;
          Johne of the Park rypis kist and ark,
          For all sic wark he is rycht meit.

10   He is weill kend Johnne of the Syde,
          A gritter theif did never ryd,
          He never tyris for to brek byris,
          Ouir muir and myris, ouir gude a gyd.

11   Thair is ane callit Clemmettis Hob
          Fra ilk pure wiff revis thair wob
          And all the laif, quhat ever thai haif;
          The deill ressaif thairfoir his gob.

12   To se sa grit stouthe quha wald trow it,
          Onles sum grit man it allowit;
          Rycht sair I rew thocht it be trew,
          Thair is sa few that dar avow it.

13   Off sum grit men thai have sic gait,
          That reddie ar thame to debait
          And will upweir thair stollin geir,
          That nane dar steir thame air nor lait.

14   Quhat causis thevis us ouirgang
          Bot want of justice us amang.
          Nane takis cair; thocht all forfair,
          Na man will spair now to do wrang.

15   Off stouthe now thocht thae cum gud speid
          That nowder of god nor man hes dreid
          Yit, or I de, sum sall thame se
          Hing on a tre, quhill thai be deid.

spulye despoil   *pure* poor   *spune* spoon   *speit* spit
boustar bolster   *sark* shirt   *rypis kist* searches chest   *meit* fit
weill kend well known   *brek byris* break down houses   *myris* mires
wob web   *gob* mouth   *stouthe* theft   *upweir* defend   *forfair* perish

Solace in Age

1   Thocht that this warld be verie strange
    And thevis hes done my rowmes range
    And teymd my fald,
    Yit wald I leif and byd ane change
    Thocht I be ald.

2   Now me to spulyie sum not spairis,
    To tak my geir no captane cairis,
    Thai ar so bald,
    Yit tyme may cum may mend my sairis
    Thocht I be ald.

3   Sum now be force of men of weir
    My hous, my landis and my geir
    Fra me thai hald;
    Yit as I may sall mak gud cheir
    Thocht I be ald.

4   Sa weill is kend my innocence
    That I will not for none offence
    Flyt lyke ane skald,
    Bot thank god and tak patience,
    For I am ald.

5   For eild and my infirmite
    Warme claythis ar bettir for me
    To keip fra cald
    Nor in Dame Venus chamber be,
    Now being ald.

6   Off Venus play past is the heit
    For I may not the mistiris beit
    Off Meg nor Mald;
    For ane young las I am not meit,
    I am sa ald.

---

rowmes lands   *teymd* emptied   *fald* fold   *spulyie* despoil
geir possessions   *flyt* quarrel   *skald* shrew   *eild* age
mistiris beit needs satisfy   *meit* fit

7 The fairast wenche in all this toun,
 Thocht I hir had in hir best gown
 Rycht braiflie braild,
 Withe hir I mycht not play the loun
 I am so ald.

8 My wyff sum tyme wald telis trow
 And mony lesingis weill allow
 War of me tald;
 Scho will not eyndill on me now
 And I sa ald.

9 My hors, my harnes and my speir
 And all uther my hoisting geir
 Now may be sald;
 I am not habill for the weir,
 I am so ald.

10 Quhone young men cumis fra the grene
 At the futball playing had bene
 With brokin spald,
 I thank my god I want my ene
 And am so ald.

11 Thocht I be sweir to ryd or gang
 Thair is sum thing I wantit lang
 Fane have I wald
 And thame puneist that did me wrang,
 Thocht I be ald.

braild arrayed *loun* lecher
telis trow believe tales *lesingis* lies *eyndill* be jealous of
hoisting campaigning *spald* collar-bone *sweir* unwilling

Robert Sempill

The Ballat maid upoun Margret Fleming, Callit the Flemyng Bark in Edinburght

1   I haif a littill Fleming berge,
    Off clenkett work bot scho is wicht;
    Quhat pylett takis my schip in chairge
    Mon hald hir clynlie, trym and ticht,
    Se that hir hatchis be handlit richt
    With steirburd, baburd, luf and lie,
    Scho will sale all the winter nicht
    And nevir tak a telyevie.

2   With evin keill befoir the wind
    Scho is richt fairdy with a saill
    Bot at ane lufe scho lyis behind;
    Gar heiss hir quhill hir howbands skaill,
    Draw weill the takill to hir taill,
    Scho will nocht miss to lay your mast,
    To pomp als oft as ye may haill,
    Yeill nevir hald hir watterfast.

3   To calfet hir oft can do non ill
    And talloun quhair the fludmark flowis,
    But gif scho lekkis, gett men of skill
    To stop hir hoilis laich in the howiss;
    For falt of hemp tak hary towis,
    With stane ballest withouttin uder.
    In moneless nichtis it is na mowis
    Except ane stout man steir hir ruder.

clenkett riveted   *trym* firmly   *ticht* tight
baburd, luf and lie larboard, windward and leeward   *telyevie* pitch
fairdy swift   *heiss* hoist   *howbands skaill* hough-bands separate
pomp pump   *haill* haul   *calfet* caulk   *talloun* cover with tallow
lekkis leaks   *laich* low   *howiss* holds   *towis* ropes   *mowis* sport

4   A fair veschell abone the watter
         And is bot laitly reiket to,
         Quhairto till deif you with tome clatter
         Ar nane sic in the floit as scho.
         Plum weill the grund, quhat evir ye doo,
         Haill on the fuk-scheit and the blind,
         Scho will tak in at cap and koo
         Without scho ballast be behind.

5   Na pedderis pak scho will ressaif
         Althocht hir travell scho sould tyne,
         Na coukcald karle nor carllingis pet
         That dois thair corne and caitell cryne,
         Bot quhair scho finds a fallow fyne
         He wilbe fraucht fre for a souss;
         Scho kareis nocht bot men and wyne
         And bulyoun to the counye-houss.

6   For merchandmen I may haif mony
         But nane sic as I wald desyre
         And I am layth to mell with ony
         To leif my mater in the myre,
         That man that wirks best for his hyre,
         Syne he salbe my mariner,
         Bot nycht and day mon he nocht tyre
         That sailis my bony ballinger.

7   For ankerhald nane can be fund,
         I pray you cast the leidlyne out
         And gif ye can nocht get the grund,
         Steir be the compas and keip hir rout;
         Syne treveiss still and lay about
         And gar hir top tuiche wind and waw;
         Quhair anker dryvis thair is na dout
         Thir tripand tyddis may tyne us aw.

reiket rigged   *tome clatter* empty noise
fuk-scheit mainsail   *blind* spritsail   *cap* prow   *koo* stern
pedderis pedlar's   *tyne* lose   *carllingis* old woman's   *cryne* shrink
fraucht carried   *souss* plunge   *bulyoun* bullion   *counye-houss* mint
ballinger small vessel   *leidlyne* sounding line   *rout* route
treveiss tack against wind   *waw* wave   *tripand tyddis* rapid tides

8   Now is my pretty pynnege reddy,
       Abydand on sum merchand blok;
       Bot be scho emptie, be our leddy,
       Scho will be kittill of hir dok.
       Scho will ressaif na landwart Jok,
       Thocht he wald fraught hir for a croun;
       Thus fare ye weill, sayis gude Johnne Cok,
       Ane nobill telyeour in this toun.

---

pynnege pinnace   *merchand b lok* commercial bargain
kittill touchy   *dok* stern
landwart Jok country bumpkin   *fraught* load

Alexander Montgomerie

The Cherrie and the Slae

1   About a bank with balmie bewes,
Where nightingals their nots renews
With gallant goldspinks gay,
The mavise, mirle and Progne proud,
The lintwhite, lark and laverock loud,
Saluted mirthful May:
When Philomel had sweetly sung,
To Progne she deplored
How Tereus cut out her tongue
And falsely her deflorde;
Which storie, so sorie,
To shew ashamd she seemde,
To heare her, so neare her,
I doubted if I dream'd.

2   The cushat crouds, the corbie cries,
The cuckow couks, the pratling pyes
To geck her they begin.
The jargoun of the jangling jayes,
The craiking crawes, the keckling kayes,
They deav'd me with their din.
The painted pawne with Argoes eyes,
Can on his mayock cal,
The turtle wailes on withered trees,
And Echo answered all,
Repeiting, with greiting,
How faire Narcissus fell,
By lying, and spying,
His shadow in the well.

---

slae sloe   *bewes* boughs   *goldspinks* goldfinches   *mirle* blackbird
Progne Swallow   *lintwhite* linnet   *laverock* skylark
Philomel Nightingale   *cushat* wood pigeon   *crouds* coos
corbie raven   *pyes* magpies   *geck* mock
keckling kayes cackling jackdaws   *deav'd* deafened   *pawne* peacock
mayock mate

3 I saw the hurcheon and the hare,
    In hidlings hirpling heere and there,
    To mak their morning mange;
    The con, the conny and the cat,
    Whese dainty dounes with dew were wat,
    With stiffe mustaches strang;
    The hart, the hynd, the dae, the rae,
    The fulmart and false foxe;
    The bearded buck clamb up the brae
    With birsie baires and brocks.
    Some feeding, some dreading,
    The hunters subtile snares,
    With skipping and tripping,
    They plaid them all in paires.

4 The aire was sober, soft and sweet,
    But mistie vapours, wind and weet,
    But quyet, calme and cleare,
    To foster Floras fragrant flowres,
    Whereon Apollos paramours
    Had trinckled many a teare;
    The which like silver shakers shynde,
    Imbrodering beauties bed,
    Wherewith their heavy heads declinde,
    In Mayes colours cled:
    Some knopping, some dropping,
    Of balmie liquor sweet,
    Excelling, in smelling,
    Through Phoebus wholsome heat.

5 Mee thought an heavenly heartsome thing,
    Where dew like diamonds did hing,
    Ou'r twinckling all the trees,
    To study on the flourishde twists,
    Admiring natures alcumists,
    Laborious busie bees;

---

hurcheon hedgehog *hidlings* secret places
mange chorus *con* squirrel *conny* rabbit *dae* doe *rae* roe
fulmart pole-cat *clamb* climbed *brae* hillside *birsie* bristly
brocks badgers *imbrodering* embroidering *knopping* budding
heartsome pleasant *flourishde twists* blossomed twigs

Whereof some sweetest hony sought
To stay their lives to sterve,
And some the waxie vessels wrought,
Their purchase to preserve.
So heaping for keeping,
It in their hyves they hide;
Precisely, and wisely,
For winter they provide.

6   To pen the pleasures of that parke,
How every blossome, branch, and bark
Against the sun did shine,
I passe to poets to compile
In high, heroick, stately stile,
Whose Muse surmatches mine;
But as I looked mine alone,
I saw a river rinne
Out ou'r a steepie rock of stone,
Syne lighted in a linne;
With tumbling, and rumbling,
Amongst the roches round,
Devalling, and falling,
Into a pit profound.

7   Through routing of the river rang
The roches, sounding like a sang,
Where descant did abound.
With treble, tenor, counter, meene,
An echo blew a basse between
In diapason sound,
Set with the C-sol-fa-uth cleife
With long and large at list,
With quaver, crotchet, semi-briefe
And not a minim mist;

to stay their lives to sterve prevent themselves from starving
surmatches surpasses   *linne* waterfall   *devalling* descending
routing roaring   *meene* intermediate part   *diapason* musical harmony
cleife clef   *at list* at one's pleasure

Compleetly and sweetly,
She firdound flat and sharp,
Than Muses, which uses
To pin Apollos harpe.

8   Who would have tyr'd to heare that tone,
     Which birds corroborate ay abone
     With layes of lovesome larks;
     Which climb so high in christal skyes,
     While Cupid wakned with the cryes
     Of natures chappel clarks;
     Who, leaving al the heavens above,
     Alighted on the eard?
     Lo, how that little Lord of love
     Before me there appeard,
     So mild-like, and child-like,
     With bow three quarters skant,
     Syne moylie, and coylie,
     Hee looked like a sant.

9   A cleanly crispe hang over his eyes,
     His quaver by his naked thyes
     Hang in a silver lace;
     Of gold betweene his shoulders grew
     Two pretty wings wherewith he flew,
     On his left arme a brace.
     This god soone off his geare he shook
     Upon the grassie ground:
     I ran as lightly for to looke,
     Where ferlies might be found.
     Amazed, I gazed
     To see his geare so gay;
     Perceiving mine having,
     He counted mee his prey.

firdound warbled   *abone* above
moylie demurely   *sant* saint   *cleanly* neat   *crispe* gauze veil
lace cord   *brace* wrist-guard   *ferlies* wonders   *having* behaviour

10   His youth and stature made mee stout;
        Of doublenesse I had no doubt
        But bourded with my boy.
        Quoth I, "How call they thee my child?"
        "Cupido sir," quoth he and smilde.
        "Please you mee to imploy,
        For I can serve you in your sute
        If you please to impire,
        With wings to flee and shafts to shute
        Or flames to set on fire.
        Make choise then, of those then,
        Or of a thousand things;
        But crave them and have them."
        With that I woo'd his wings.

11   "What would thou give, my heart," quoth he,
        "To have these wanton wings to flee,
        To sporr thy sprite a while?
        Or what if love should send thee heere,
        Bow, quaver, shafts and shooting geare,
        Somebody to beguile?"
        "This geare," quoth I, "cannot be bought,
        Yet I would have it faine."
        "What if," quoth he, "it cost thee nought
        But rendring all againe?"
        His wings then, he brings then,
        And band them on my back.
        "Goe flye now," quoth he now,
        And so my leave I take.

12   I sprang up with Cupido's wings,
        Whose shots and shooting geare resignes,
        To lend me for a day.
        As Icarus with borrowed flight,
        I mounted higher than I might,
        Ou'r perilous a play.

bourded jested   *impire* command   *sporr* spur
play venture

First foorth I drew the double dart,
Which sometimes shot his mother,
Wherewith I hurt my wanton heart
In hope to hurt another.
It hurt me, or burnt mee,
While either end I handle;
Come see now, in mee now,
The butterflee and candle.

13   As she delites into the low,
So was I browden of my bow,
As ignorant as she;
And as she flyes while she is fir'de,
So with the dart that I desirde,
Mine hands hath hurt mee to.
As foolish Phaeton by sute,
His fathers chaire obtainde,
I longed in loves bow to shoote,
Not marking what it mean'de.
More wilful, than skilful,
To flee I was so fond,
Desiring, impyring,
And so was seene upond.

14   Too late I knew, who hewes too high,
The spaile shall fall into his eye,
Too late I went to schooles,
Too late I heard the swallow preach,
Too late Experience doth teach –
The schoole-master of fooles.
Too late I find the nest I seek,
When all the birds are flowne,
Too late the stable doore I steeke,
When as the steede is stowne.
Too late ay, their state ay,
As foolish folk espy;
Behind so, they finde so,
Remead, and so doe I.

low flame   *browden* enamoured   *sute* entreaty
upond upon it   *hewes* raises himself   *spaile* splinter
steeke shut   *stowne* stolen   *remead* cure

15 If I had ripely beene advisde,
   I had not rashly enterprisde
   To soare with borrowed pens,
   Nor yet had sayde the archer-craft
   To shoot myselfe with such a shaft,
   As Reason quite miskens.
   Fra Wilfulnes gave me my wound,
   I had no force to flee;
   Then came I groning to the ground.
   "Friend, welcome home," quoth he.
   "Where flew you? Whom slew yee?
   Or who brings home the booting?
   I see now," quoth he now,
   "Ye have beene at the shooting."

16 As scorne comes commonly with skaith,
   So I behovde to bide them baith,
   So staggering was my state,
   That under cure I got such check,
   Which I might not remove nor neck,
   But either staile or mait.
   Mine agony was so extreame,
   I swelt and swound for feare.
   But ere I wakned off my dreame,
   He spoild me of my geare.
   With flight then, on hight then,
   Sprang Cupid in the skyes,
   Forgetting, and setting
   At nought my carefull cries.

17 So long with sight I followed him,
   While both my dazeled eyes grew dimme
   Through staring of the starnes;
   Which flew so thick before mine eyne,
   Some red, some yellow, blew and greene,
   Which troubled all mine harnes,
   That every thing appeared two
   To my barbuilied braine;

pens feathers
miskens is ignorant of *booting* booty *skaith* harm
behovde to bide had to endure *nor neck* prevent being checked
but without *staile* stale *mait* mate *while* until
starnes stars *harnes* brains *barbuilied* muddled

But long might I lye looking so
Ere Cupid came againe;
Whose thundring, with wondring,
I heard up through the aire.
Through clouds so, he thuddes so
And flew I wist not where.

18   Then when I saw that god was gone
And I in langour left alone
And sore tormented too,
Sometime I sigh'd while I was sad,
Sometime I musde, and most gone mad;
I doubted what to doe.
Sometime I rav'd halfe in a rage
As one into despare,
To be opprest with such a page,
Lord, if my heart was saire!
Like Dido, Cupido,
I widdle and I wary,
Who reft mee, and left mee,
In such a feirie farie.

19   Then felt I Courage and Desire
Inflame mine heart with uncouth fire,
To me before unknowne.
But then no blood in me remaines
Unburnt or boyld within my braines
By loves bellowes blowne.
To drowne it ere I was devorit
With sighs I went about;
But ay the more I shoope to smor it
The bolder it brake out,
Ay preasing, but ceasing,
While it might break the bounds;
Mine hew so, foorth shew so,
The dolour of my wounds.

widdle fret
wary curse   *feirie farie* confused state of mind   *uncouth* unknown
smor it tried to put it out   *preasing* striving   *hew* complexion

20   With deadly visage, pale and wan,
        More like an atomie than man,
        I withered cleane away.
        As waxe before the fire, I felt
        Mine heart within my bosome melt,
        And piece and piece decay.
        My veines by brangling like to break
        My punses lap with pith,
        So fervency did mee infect
        That I was vext therewith.
        Mine heart ay, it start ay,
        The firie flames to flee;
        Ay howping, through lowping,
        To leape at libertie.

21   But O, alas, it was abusde!
        My carefull corps kept it inclusde
        In prison of my breast,
        With sighs so sopped and ou'rset,
        Like to a fish fast in a net,
        In deadthraw undeceast;
        Which though in vaine, it strives by strength
        For to pul out her head,
        Which profites nothing at the length,
        But hastning to her dead;
        With thristing and wristing,
        The faster still is sho;
        There I so, did lye so,
        My death advancing to.

22   The more I wrestled with the wind,
        The faster stil my selfe I finde;
        No mirth my minde could mease.
        More noy than I had never none,
        I was so alterd and ou'rgone
        Through drouth of my disease.
        Yet weakly, as I might, I raise,
        My sight grew dimme and dark;

---

atomie skeleton   *brangling* shaking   *punses lap* pulses leaped
howping hoping   *sopped* drenched in tears   *ou'rset* weary
deadthraw death struggle   *thristing* thrusting   *wristing* straining
mease calm   *noy* pain

I staggered at the windling strayes,
No token I was stark.
Both sightles and mightles,
I grew almost at once;
In anguish I languish,
With many grievous groanes.

23   With sober pace yet I approach
Hard to the river and the roch,
Whereof I spake before;
The river such a murmure made,
As to the sea it softly slade;
The craige was stay and shore.
Then Pleasure did me so provoke
There partly to repaire,
Betwixt the river and the rocke,
Where Hope grew with Despare.
A tree then, I see then,
Of Cherries on the braes.
Below too, I saw too,
A bush of bitter Slaes.

24   The Cherries hang above mine head,
Like trickling rubies round and red,
So high up in the heugh;
Whose shadowes in the rivers shew,
As graithly glansing as they grew
On trembling twists and teugh,
Whiles bow'd through burden of their birth,
Declining downe their tops.
Reflexe of Phoebus off the firth,
Now coloured all their knoppes;
With dancing and glancing,
In tirle as Dornick champe;
Which streamed and leamed,
Through lightnes of that lampe.

windling strayes slightest things
no token in no way   *roch* rock   *slade* flowed   *heugh* crag
graithly glansing clearly shining   *teugh* tough   *knoppes* buds
tirle ripple   *Dornick champe* ground of piece of embroidery
leamed shone

25 With earnest eye while I espy
   That fruite betwixt me and the skye,
   Halfe gate almost to heaven;
   The craige so cumbersome to climb,
   The tree so tall of growth and trim
   As any arrow even;
   I calde to minde how Daphne did
   Within the laurel shrinke,
   When from Apollo she her hid,
   A thousand times I thinke.
   That tree there, to mee there,
   As shee his laurel thought,
   Aspyring, but tyring,
   To get that fruite I sought.

26 To climb that craige it was no buite,
   Let bee to prease to pul the fruite
   In top of all the tree;
   I know no way whereby to come,
   By any craft to get it clum,
   Appearandly to mee.
   The craige was ugly, stay and dreigh,
   The tree long, sound and small;
   I was affraide to climb so high,
   For feare to fetch a fall.
   Affrayed, I stayed,
   And looked up aloft.
   Whiles minting, whiles stinting,
   My purpose changed oft.

27 Then Dread with Danger and Despare
   Forbade me minting any mare,
   To raxe above my reach.
   "What? Tush!" quoth Courage, "Man go to,
   He is but daft that hath to doe
   And spares for everie speach,
   For I have oft heard sooth men say,
   And we may see't ourselves,

---

gate way *buite* remedy *clum* climbed
stay steep *dreigh* tedious
whiles minting, whiles stinting now striving, now holding back
Danger coyness *minting* trying *raxe* stretch

That Fortune helps the hardie ay
And pultrons ay repels.
Then care not and feare not,
Dread, Danger nor Despare;
To fazards, hard hazards,
Is death or they come there.

28   "Who speeds but such as high aspyres?
Who triumphs not, but such as tyres
To win a noble name?
Of shrinking what but shame succeeds?
Then doe as thou would have thy deeds
In register of fame.
I put the case thou not prevailde,
So thou with honour die,
Thy life but not thy courage failde,
Shal poets pen of thee.
Thy name then, from Fame then,
Can never be cut aff;
Thy grave ay shal have ay
That honest epitaph.

29   "What canst thou losse when honour lives?
Renowne thy vertue ay revives,
If valiantly thou end."
Quoth Danger, "Huly, friend, take head;
Untimous spurring spilles the stead;
Take tent what yee pretend.
Thogh Courage counsel thee to climb,
Beware thou kep no skaith;
Have thou na helpe, but Hope and him,
They may beguile thee baith.
Thysell now can tell now
The counsel of these clarkes;
Wherethrow yet, I trow yet,
Thy breast doth beare the marks.

---

pultrons cowards   *fazards* weaklings   *speeds* succeeds   *huly* slowly
untimous untimely   *tent* care   *skaith* harm

30   "Burnt bairne with fire the danger dreads,
        So I believe thy bosome bleeds,
        Since last that fire thou felt:
        Besides that seindle times thou sees,
        That ever Courage keeps the keyes
        Of knowledge at his belt.
        Though he bid fordward with the gunnes,
        Smal powder he provides;
        Be not a novice of that nunnes,
        Who saw not both the sides;
        Fooles haste ay, almaist ay,
        Ou'rsyles the sight of some,
        Who luikes not, or huikes not,
        What afterward may come.

31   "Yet Wisedome wisheth thee to wey
        This figure in Philosophy,
        A lesson worth to leare,
        Which is in time for to take tent
        And not when time is past repent
        And buy repentance deare.
        Is there no honour after life
        Except thou slay thy sel?
        Wherefore hath Atropus that knife?
        I trow thou canst not tell.
        Who but it, would cut it,
        Which Clotho scarce hath spun;
        Destroying the joying,
        Before it be begun.

32   "All ou'rs are repute to be vice,
        Ou'r high, ou'r low, ou'r rash, ou'r nice,
        Ou'r hote, or yet ou'r cold;
        Thou seemes unconstant by thy signes,
        Thy thought is on a thousand things,
        Thou wats not what thou would.
        Let Fame her pitty on thee powre,
        When all thy bones are broken;

---

seindle seldom   *ou'rsyles* beguiles   *huikes* takes into account
leare learn   *ou'rs* excesses   *nice* fastidious   *wats* knows

Yon Slae, suppose thou think it sowre,
Would satisfie to sloken
Thy drouth now, of youth now,
Which dries thee with desire;
Assuage then, thy rage then,
Foule water quencheth fire.

33   "What foole art thou to die a thrist,
And now may quench it if thou list,
So easily but paine?
More honour is to vanquish ane,
Than fight with tensome and be tane,
And either hurt or slay[ne];
The practick is to bring to passe
And not to enterprise,
And as good drinking out of glasse
As gold in any wise.
I lever have ever
A fowle in hand or tway,
Then seeing ten flying
About me all the day.

34   "Looke where thou lights before thou loupe,
And slip no certainty for Hope,
Who guides thee but be gesse."
Quoth Courage, "Cowards take no cure
To sit with shame, so they be sure;
I like them all the lesse.
What pleasure purchast is but paine,
Or honour won with ease?
He wil not lye where he is slaine,
Who doubts before he dies.
For feare then, I heare then,
But onely one remead,
Which lattis, and that is
For to cut off the head.

---

sloken slake	*list* wish	*tensome* ten at once	*practick* practice
lever rather	*lights* lands	*loupe* leap *cure* care	*lattis* prevents

35   "What is the way to heale thine hurt?
        What way is there to stay thy sturt?
        What meanes to make thee merrie?
        What is the comfort that thou craves?
        Suppose these sophists thee deceaves,
        Thou knowes it is the Cherrie.
        Since for it onely thou but thirsts,
        The Slae can bee no buite.
        In it also thine health consists
        And in none other fruite.
        Why quakes thou and shakes thou
        Or studies at our strife?
        Advise thee, it lyes thee,
        On no lesse than thy life.

36   "If any patient would be pansde,
        Why should he loupe when he is lansde,
        Or shrinke when he is shorne?
        For I have heard chirurgians say,
        Oft-times deferring of a day
        Might not be mend the morne.
        Take time in time ere time be tint,
        For time will not remaine.
        What forceth fire out of the flint,
        But as hard match againe?
        Delay not, nor fray not,
        And thou shall see it sa:
        Such gets ay, as sets ay,
        Stout stomackes to the brae.

37   "Though all beginning be most hard,
        The end is pleasant afterward;
        Then shrinke not for no showre;
        When once that thou thy greening get,
        Thy paine and travel is forget,
        The sweete exceeds the sowre.
        Goe to then quickly, feare no thir,
        For Hope good hap hath height."

---

sturt trouble   *buite* remedy   *studies* perplexes yourself   *lyes* concerns
pansde healed   *loupe* leap   *chirurgians* surgeons   *tint* lost
fray fear   *brae* hillside   *greening* longing   *thir* those
height promised

Quoth Danger, "Be not sudden, sir;
The matter is of weight.
First spy both, then try both,
Advisement doth none ill:
Thou may then, I say then,
Be wilful when thou will.

38   "But yet to minde the proverbe call,
'Who uses perils perish shal:'
Short while their life them lasts."
"And I have heard," quoth Hope, "that he
Should never shape to saile the sea,
That for all perils casts.
How many through Despare are dead,
That never perils priev'd!
How many also, if thou read,
Of lives have we releiv'd?
Who being, even dying,
But Danger but desparde;
A hunder, I wonder,
But thou hast heard declarde.

39   "If we two hold not up thine heart,
Which is the chiefe and noblest part,
Thy works would not goe well;
Considering the companions can
Dissuade a silly, simple man
To hazard for his heale.
Suppose they have deceived some
Ere we and they might meete,
They get not credance where we come,
In any man of spreit.
By reason, their treason,
By us is plainely spyde;
Revealing, their dealing,
Which dow not be denyde.

---

shape try   *priev'd* tested   *hunder* hundred
heale wellbeing   *spreit* spirit

40 "With sleekie sophismes seeming sweete,
  As all their doing were discreet,
   They wish thee to be wise;
  Postponing time from houre to houre,
  But faith, in underneath the flowre
   The lurking serpent lyes.
  Suppose thou seest her not a stime,
   While that she sting thy foote;
  Perceives thou not what precious time,
   Thy sleuth doth overshoote?
    Alas man, thy case man,
    In lingring I lament:
    Goe to now, and doe now,
    That Courage be content.

41 "What if Melancholy come in
  And get a grip ere thou begin?
   Then is thy labour lost,
  For he will hold thee hard and fast,
  Til time and place and fruite be past,
   And thou give up the ghost.
  Then shal be graven upon that place,
   Which on thy tombe is laid,
  'Sometime there liv'd such one.' Alas,
   But how shal it bee said?
    'Heere lyes now, but prise now,
    Into dishonours bed,
    A cowart, as thou art,
    Who from his fortune fled.'

42 "Imagine man, if thou were laid
  In grave, and syne might heare this said,
   Would thou not sweat for shame?
  Yes faith, I doubt not but thou would;
  Therefore if thou have eyes behold,
   How they would smore thy fame.
  Goe to and make no more excuse
   Ere life and honour losse,
  And either them or us refuse;

stime particle *sleuth* sloth *prise* renown

There is no other chose.
Consider, togidder,
That we doe never dwell;
At length ay, but strength ay,
The pultrons we expell."

43   Quoth Danger, "Since I understand,
That counsell can be no command,
I have no more to say;
Except if that you thinke it good,
Take counsel yet ere ye conclude,
Of wiser men then they.
They are but rackles, young and rash,
Suppose they thinke us fleit;
If of our fellowship ye fash,
Goe with them hardly be it.
God speed you, they lead you,
Who have not meekle wit.
Expel us, yeeil tell us,
Heerafter comes not yit."

44   While Danger and Despare retir'de,
Experience came in and spear'de
What all the matter meande;
With him came Reason, Wit and Skill.
Then they began to aske at Will,
"Where make you to, my friend?"
"To pluck yon lustie Cherrie, loe,"
Quoth he, "and quyte the Slae."
Quoth they, "Is there no more adoe
Ere yee win up the brae,
But doe it, and to it,
Perforce your fruite to pluck?
Well brother, some other
Were better to conduct.

45   "We grant yee may be good enough
But yet the hazard of yon heugh
Requyres a graver guide.
As wise as yee are may goe wrang;

---

fleit scared   *fash* are troubled   *hardly* boldly
meekle much   *spear'de* asked   *quyte* leave   *heugh* crag

Therefore take counsell ere ye gang
Of some that stands beside.
But who were yon three yee forbade
Your company right now?"
Quoth Wil, "Three preachers to persuade
The poysonde Slae to pull.
They tratled and pratled
A long halfe hour and mare;
Foul fal them! They call them
Dread, Danger and Despare.

46   "They are more fashious than of feck,
Yon fazards durst not for their neck,
Climb up the craige with us.
Fra we determined to die
Or then to climbe the Cherrie tree,
They bode about the bush.
They are conditionde like the cat,
They would not weete their feete;
But yet if any fish we gate,
They would be apt to eate.
Though they now, I say now,
To hazard have no heart;
Yet luck we or pluck wee
The fruite they would not part.

47   "But when we get our voyage wun,
They shal not then a Cherrie cun,
Who would not enterprise."
"Well," quoth Experience, "ye boast;
But he that reckon'd but his hoast,
Oftimes he counteth twise.
Ye sell the baires skin on his back
But bide while ye it get;
When ye have done, its time to crack;
Ye fish before the net.
What haste sir, ye taste sir,
The Cherrie ere yee pow it;
Beware sir, ye are sir,
More talkative nor trowit."

---

tratled tattled   *fashious* annoying   *feck* value   *fazards* weaklings
bode stayed   *cun* taste   *crack* boast   *pow* pull
nor trowit than believed

48   "Call Danger back againe," quoth Skil,
"To see what he can say to Wil,
We see him shoad so straite;
We may not trow what each one tels."
Quoth Courage, "We concluded els,
He serves not for our mate,
For I can tel you al perquiere
His counsel ere he come."
Quoth Hope, "Whereto should he come here?
He cannot hold him dum.
He speaks ay, and seeks ay
Delayes oft times and drifts,
To grieve us, and dieve us
With sophistrie and shifts."

49   Quoth Reason, "Why was he debarde?
The tale is ill cannot be heard,
Yet let us heare him anes."
Then Danger to declare began,
How Hope and Courage tooke the man
To leade him all their lanes;
How they would have him up the hill,
But either stoppe or stay,
And who was welcomer than Will,
He would be foremost ay.
He could doe, and should doe,
Who ever would or nought.
Such speeding, proceeding,
Unlikely was I thought.

50   "Therefore I wisht him to beware
And rashly not to run ou'r far,
Without such guides as yee."
Quoth Courage, "Friend I heare you faile,
Take better tent unto your tale,
Ye said it could not bee.
Besides that ye would not consent,
That ever we should clim."

---

perquiere exactly   *dieve* deafen   *their lanes* on their own
stay hindrance   *faile* speak falsely

Quoth Wil, "For my part I repent,
We saw them more than him;
For they are the stayare
Of us as well as hee;
I thinke now, they shrinke now:
Goe forward, let them bee.

51   "Goe, goe, we nothing doe but guckes;
They say the voyage never luckes,
Where each one hath a vote."
Quoth Wisedome gravely, "Sir, I grant
We were no worse your vote to want,
Some sentence now I note.
Suppose you speake it but be gesse,
Some fruite therein I finde;
Ye would be foremost I confesse
But comes oft-times behind.
It may be that they bee,
Deceiv'd that never doubted;
Indeed sir, that head sir,
Hath meekle wit about it."

52   Then wilful Will began to rage
And swore he saw nothing in age
But anger, yre and grudge.
"And for myselfe," quoth he, "I sweare
To quyte all my companions heere,
If they admit you judge.
Experience is growne so old,
That he begins to rave;
The rest but Courage are so cold
No hazarding they have;
For Danger, farre stranger,
Hath made them than they were;
Goe fra them, we pray them,
Who neither dow nor dare.

---

guckes talk foolishly   *luckes* is fortunate
sentence sense   *quyte* leave   *stranger* stronger

53 "Why may not wee three leade this one?
   I led an hundreth mine alone
   But counsel of them all."
   "I grant," quoth Wisedome, "ye have led;
   But I would speere how many sped
   Or furthered but a fall?
   But either few or none, I trow,
   Experience can tell.
   He sayes that man may wite but you,
   The first time that hee fell;
   He kens then, whose pens then,
   Thou borrowed him to flee.
   His wounds yet, which stounds yet,
   He got them then through thee."

54 "That," quoth Experience, "is true.
   Will flattered him when first he flew,
   Wil set him in a low,
   Will was his counsell and convoy,
   Will borrowed from the blinded boy
   Both quaver, wings and bow;
   Wherewith before he say'd to shoote,
   He neither yeeld to youth,
   Nor yet had need of any fruite,
   To quench his deadly drouth;
   Which pines him, and dwines him,
   To death, I wot not how:
   If Will then, did ill then,
   Himselfe remembers now.

55 "For I, Experience, was there,
   Like as I use to bee all where,
   What time hee wited Will
   To be the ground of all his griefe,
   As I my selfe can bee a priefe
   And witnes thereuntill.
   There are no bounds but I have beene,
   Nor hidlings from mee hid,
   Nor secret things but I have seene,
   That hee or any did.

speere ask *sped* succeeded *wite* blame *pens* feathers
stounds ache *say'd* tried *dwines* washes away *wited* blamed
priefe witness

Therefore now, no more now,
Let him thinke to conceal it;
For why now, even I now,
Am debtbound to reveal it."

56 "My custome is for to declare
The truth, and neither eke nor paire
For any man a joate:
If wilful Will delytes in lyes,
Example in thy selfe thou sees,
How he can turne his coate,
And with his language would allure
Thee yet to breake thy bones.
Thou knowes thyself if he be sure;
Thou usde his counsell ones.
Who would yet, behold yet,
To wreak thee were not wee.
Thinke on you, on yon now,"
Quoth Wisedome then to mee.

57 "Wel," quoth Experience, "if hee
Submits himselfe to you and mee,
I wote what I should say:
Our good advise he shall not want,
Providing alwayes that hee grant
To put yon Will away,
And banish both him and Despare,
That all good purpose spils;
So he will mell with them no mare,
Let them two flyte their fils.
Such cossing, but lossing,
All honest men may use."
"That change now, were strange now,"
Quoth Reason, "to refuse."

58 Quoth Will, "Fy on him when he flew,
That powde not Cherries then anew
For to have staide his hurt."
Quoth Reason, "Though he beare the blame,
He never saw nor needed them, .

eke enlarge *joate* jot *spils* destroys
mell mingle *flyte* scold *cossing* exchanging

While he himselfe had hurt.
First when he mistred not, he might,
He needs and may not now;
Thy folly, when he had his flight,
Empashed him to pow;
Both hee now, and we now,
Perceives thy purpose plaine,
To turne him, and burne him,
And blow on him againe."

59 Quoth Skil, "What would wee longer strive?
Far better late than never thrive.
Come let us helpe him yit.
Tint time we may not get againe,
We waste but present time in vaine."
"Beware with that," quoth Wit.
"Speake on, Experience, let see;
We think you hold you dumb."
"Of bygones I have heard," quoth he,
"I know not things to come."
Quoth Reason, "The season,
With slouthing slydes away.
First take him, and make him
A man if that you may."

60 Quoth Will, "If he be not a man,
I pray you sirs what is he than?
He lookes like one at least."
Quoth Reason, "If he follow thee,
And minde not to remaine with mee,
Nought but a bruital beast.
A man in shape doth nought consist,
For all your tanting tales;
Therefore, sir Will, I would yee wist
Your Metaphysick failes.
Goe leare yet, a yeare yet,
Your Logick at the schooles,
Some day then, yee may then
Passe master with the mules."

mistred needed *empashed* hindered
tint lost *slouthing* slothfulness
tanting taunting *leare* learn

61   Quoth Will, "I marvel what you meane;
             Should I not trow mine own two eyne
             For all your Logick schooles?
             If I did not, I were not wise."
             Quoth Reason, "I have told you thrise,
             None ferlies more than fooles;
             There be more senses than the sight,
             Which ye ou'rhaile for haste.
             To wit, if ye remember right,
             Smel, hearing, touch and taste.
             All quick things have sic things,
             I meane both man and beast,
             By kinde ay, we finde ay,
             Few lackes them at the least.

62   "So by that consequence of thine,
             Or syllogisme said like a swine,
             A kow may learne thee laire.
             Thou uses onely but the eyes;
             She touches, tastes, smels, heares and sees,
             Which matches thee and maire.
             But since no triumph yee intend,
             As presently appeares,
             Sir, for your clergie to be kend,
             Take yee two asses eares.
             No miter, perfyter,
             Got Midas for his meed;
             That hood sir, is good sir,
             To hap your braine-sick head.

63   "Ye have no feele for to defyne,
             Though yee have cunning to decline
             A man to bee a moole;
             With little work, yet yee may vowde
             To grow a gallant horse and good,
             To ride thereon at Yoole.
             But to our ground where wee began,
             For all your gustlesse jests,

eyne eyes   *ferlies* wonders
quick living   *learne* teach   *laire* learning   *clergie* learning
miter dunce's cap   *hap* cover   *moole* mule   *gustlesse* tasteless

I must be master of the man
But thou to bruital beasts;
So wee two must bee two,
To cause both kinds be knowne;
Keep mine then, from thine then,
And each one use their owne."

64 Then Will, as angry as an ape,
Ran ramping, swearing rude and rape,
Saw he none other shift.
He would not want an inch his wil,
Even whether't did him good or ill,
For thirty of his thrift;
He would be formest in the field
And master if he might:
Yea, hee should rather die than yeeld,
Though Reason had the right.
"Shal he now, make mee now
His subject or his slave?
No, rather my father
Shal quick goe to the grave.

65 "I height him while mine heart is haile,
To perish first ere he prevaile,
Come after what so may."
Quoth Reason, "Doubt yee not indeed,
Yee hitte the naile upon the head;
It shall bee as yee say.
Suppose yee spur for to aspire,
Your bridle wants a bit;
That marke may leave you in the myre
As sicker as yee sit.
Your sentence, repentance,
Shall leave you I believe,
And anger you langer,
When yee that practick prieve.

---

rape hastily *thrift* position *height* promised *sicker* certain
practick exploit *prieve* undergo

66   "As yee have dyted your decreet,
    Your prophecy to bee compleat,
    Perhaps and to your paines;
    It hath beene said, and may be so,
    'A wilful man wants never woe,
    Though he get little gaines;'
    But since ye thinkt an easie thing
    To mount above the moone,
    Of your owne fiddle take a spring
    And dance when yee have done.
    If than sir, the man sir,
    Like of your mirth hee may;
    And speare first, and heare first,
    What he himselfe will say."

67   Then altogether they began
    And said, "Come on thou martyrde man,
    What is thy will, advise."
    Abasde a bony while I stood,
    And musde ere I mine answere made.
    I turnd me once or twise,
    Beholding everyone about,
    Whose motions mov'd me maist.
    Some seem'd assured, some dread for doubt,
    Will ran red-wood for haist,
    With wringing, and flinging,
    For madnes like to mang;
    Despare too, for care too,
    Would needs himselfe goe hang,

68   Which when Experience perceiv'd,
    Quoth he, "Remember if I rav'de
    As Will allegde of late,
    When as he swore nothing he saw
    In age but anger, slack and slaw,
    And cankred in conceite.
    Ye could not lucke as he alledgde,
    Who all opinions spearde.
    Hee was so frack and firie edg'd,
    He thought us foure but feard.

dyted composed *decreet* decree
spring lively tune *bony while* long time
red-wood for haist mad with rage *mang* go frantic *frack* bold

'Who panses, what chanses,'
Quoth hee, 'no worship wins;
To some best, shal come best,
Who hap wel, rack well rins.'

69   "Yet," quoth Experience, "behold,
For all the tales that ye have told,
How hee himselfe behaves;
Because Despare could come no speed,
Loe, heere he hings all but the head,
And in a widdy waves.
If you be sure, once thou may see,
To men that with them mels;
If they had hurt or helped thee,
Consider by themsels.
Then chuse thee, to use thee
By us or such as yon;
Syne soone now, have done now,
Make either off or on."

70   "Perceiv'st thou not wherefra proceeds
The frantick fantasie that feeds
Thy furious flamming fire,
Which doth thy bailfull brest combur,
That none indeed," quoth they, "can cure,
Nor helpe thine hearts desire?
The piercing passions of the spreit,
Which wastes thy vitall breath,
Doth hold thine heavy heart with heate;
Desire drawes on thy death.
Thy punces, pronunces,
All kinde of quyet rest;
That fever hath ever
Thy person so opprest.

---

panses ponders   *rack* suffering
rins endures   *widdy* willow rope
combur burn   *spreit* spirit   *punces* pulses

71 "Couldst thou come once acquaint with Skil,
  Hee knowes what humours doth thee ill
  And how thy cares contraks;
  Hee knowes the ground of all thy griefe
  And recipies of thy reliefe;
  All medicines hee maks."
  Quoth Skill, "Come on, content am I
  To put mine helping hand,
  Providing alwayes hee apply
  To counsel and command.
  While wee then," quoth he then,
  "Are minded to remaine,
  Give place now, in cace now,
  Thou get us not againe.

72 "Assure thy selfe if that we shed,
  Thou shalt not get thy purpose sped;
  Take heede, wee have thee told.
  Have done and drive not off the day;
  'The man that will not when he may,
  He shal not when hee would.'
  What wilt thou doe, I would we wist:
  Accept or give us ou'r?"
  Quoth I, "I think me more than blest
  To finde such famous foure
  Beside mee, to guide mee,
  Now when I have to doe;
  Considering what swidering
  Ye found me first into.

73 "When Courage crav'd a stomack stout
  And Danger drave mee into doubt
  With his companion Dread;
  Whiles Wil would up above the aire,
  Whiles I am drownde in deepe Despare,
  Whiles Hope held up mine head.
  Such pithie reasons and replies
  On every side they shew,
  That I, who was not very wise,
  Thought all their tales were true.

recipies prescriptions   *shed* part
swidering swithering (or hesitating)

So mony and bony,
Old problems they proponit
But quickly and likely,
I marvell meekle on it.

74   "Yet Hope and Courage wan the field,
Though Dread and Danger never yeeld,
But fled to finde refuge.
Yet when ye foure came, they were faine,
Because ye gart them come againe;
The[y] griende to get you judge.
Where they were fugitive before,
Yee made them frank and free
To speak and stand in aw no more."
Quoth Reason, "So should bee.
Oft-times now, but crymes now,
But even perforce it fals,
The strong ay, with wrong ay,
Puts weaker to the wals,

75   "Which is a fault ye must confesse.
Strength was not ordained to oppresse
With rigour by the right,
But by the contrare to sustaine
The loaden, which ou'rburthend beene,
As meckle as they might."
"So Hope and Courage did," quoth I,
"Experimented like,
Show skilde and pithy reasons why
That Danger lap the dyke."
Quoth Dreid, "Sir, take heed sir;
Long spoken part must spill;
Insist not, we wist not
Ye went against our will.

76   "With Courage ye were so content,
Ye never sought our smal consent;
Of us ye stood not aw.
Then Logick lessons ye allowit
And was determined to trow it;

---

bony excellent   *proponit* proposed   *faine* glad   *gart* made
griende longed   *meckle* much   *lap the dyke* jumped the ditch (or turf wall)

Alleageance past for law.
For all the proverbs wee perusde,
Yee thought them skantly skild;
Our reasons had beene as well rusde,
Had ye beene as well wil'de
To our side, as your side,
So truely I may tearme it;
I see now, in thee now,
Affection doth affirm't."

77   Experience then smirking smilde.
"We are no bairnes to be beguild,"
Quoth he and shooke his head;
"For authors who alledges us,
They stil would win about the bus,
To foster deadly feede;
For wee are equal for you all.
No persons wee respect.
We have been so, are yet and shall
Be found so in effect.
If we were, as ye were,
We had comde unrequyrde;
But wee now, ye see now,
Doe nothing undesirde.

78   "There is a sentence said by some,
'Let none uncald to counsell come,
That welcome weines to bee.'
Yea I have heard another yit,
'Who came uncald, unserv'd shuld sit;'
Perhaps sir, so may yee."
"Good-man, grande mercie for your gecke,"
Quoth Hope and lowly lowts;
"If yee were sent for, we suspect,
Because the doctours doubts.
Your yeares now, appeares now
With wisedome to be vext,
Rejoycing, in gloysing,
Till you have tint your text.

---

skantly skild lacking in learning   *rusde* praised   *bairnes* children
alledges cite   *bus* bush   *feede* feud   *weines* hopes
grande mercie thanks   *gecke* taunt   *lowts* bows   *gloysing* annotating
tint lost

79   "Where yee were sent for, let us see
Who would be welcomer than wee.
Prove that and we are payde."
"Wel," quoth Experience, "beware;
You know not in what case you are;
Your tongue hath you betrayde.
The man may able tine a stot,
Who cannot count his kinch;
In your owne bow you are ou'rshot
By more then halfe an inch.
Who wat sir, if that sir,
Is sowre which seemeth sweet,
I feare now, ye heare now,
A dangerous decreete.

80   "Sir, by that sentence yee have said,
I pledge ere all the play bee plaid,
That some shall lose a laike.
Since yee but put me for to prove,
Such heads as help for my behove,
Your warrand is but waike.
Speare at the man your selfe and see,
Suppose you strive for state,
If hee regrated not how hee
Had learnd my lesson late,
And granted, hee wanted
Both Reason, Wit and Skill,
Compleaning, and meaning,
Our absence did him ill.

81   "Confront him further face for face,
If yet hee rewes his rackles race,
Perhaps and ye shall heare.
For ay since Adam and since Eve,
Who first thy leasings did believe,
I sold thy doctrine deare.
What hath beene done even to this day
I keep in minde almaist;
Ye promise further than ye pay,
Sir Hope, for all your haste.

stot ox   *kinch* kine   *laike* stake   *regrated* regretted
rewes repents   *leasings* falsehoods

Promitting, unwitting,
Your heghts yee never hooked;
I show you, I know you,
Your bygones I have booked.

82   "I would, incace a count were crav'd,
Shew thousand thousands thou deceivde,
Where thou was true to one;
And by the contrare I may vant,
Which thou must (though it grieve thee) grant,
I trumped never a man,
But truely told the naked trueth
To men that meld with mee,
For neither rigour nor for rueth,
But onely loath to lie.
To some yet, to come yet,
Thy succour shall be slight;
Which I then, must try then
And register it right."

83   "Ha, ha!" quoth Hope and loudly leugh,
"Ye'r but a prentise at the pleugh,
Experience yee prieve.
Suppose all bygones as yee spacke,
Ye are no prophet worth a plack,
Nor I bound to believe.
Yee should not say sir, till yee see,
But when yee see it, say."
"Yet," quoth Experience, "at thee
Make many mints I may:
By sings now, and things now,
Which ay before mee beares,
Expressing, by gessing,
The perill that appeares."

---

promitting promising
hooked paid attention to   *booked* recorded   *count* account
vant boast   *trumped* deceived   *meld* dealt   *leugh* laughed
prentise apprentice   *pleugh* plough   *spacke* spoke   *plack* farthing
mints attacks   *sings* signs

84   Then Hope replyde, and that with pith,
          And wisely weigh'd his words therewith,
          Sententiously and short;
          Quoth hee, "I am the anchor grip,
          That saves the sailers and their ship
          From perill to their port."
          Quoth hee, "Oft times that anchor drives,
          As wee have found before,
          And loses many thousand lives
          By shipwrack on the shore.
          Your grips oft but slips oft,
          When men have most to doe,
          Syne leaves them, and reaves them
          Of my companion too.

85   "Thou leaves them not thy selfe alone,
          But to their griefe when thou art gone
          Gars Courage quite them als."
          Quoth Hope, "I would ye understood,
          I grip fast if the ground be good,
          And fleets where it is false.
          There should no fault with mee be found,
          Nor I accusde at all.
          Wyte such as should have sound the ground,
          Before the anchor fall.
          Their leede ay, at neede ay,
          Might warne them if they would;
          If they there, would stay there,
          Or have good anchor-hold.

86   "If yee read right it was not I,
          But onely Ignorance whereby
          Their carvels all were cloven.
          I am not for a trumper tane."
          "All," quoth Experience, "is ane;
          I have my processe proven,
          To wit, that we were cald each one,
          To come before wee came;

---

reaves bereaves   *quite* leave
als too   *fleets* change ground   *wyte* blame   *sound* sounded
leede ship's lead   *carvels* light vessels   *cloven* split   *trumper* deceiver
processe case

That now objection ye have none,
Your selfe may say the same.
Ye are now too farre now,
Come forward for to flee;
Perceive then, ye have then
The worst end of the tree."

87   "When Hope was gald into the quick,"
Quoth Courage, kicking at the prick,
"Wee let you well to wit:
Make hee you welcomer than wee,
Then bygones bygones, farewell he,
Except hee seeke us yit.
Hee understands his own estate,
Let him his chiftanes chuse;
But yet his battel will bee blate,
If hee our force refuse.
Refuse us, or chuse us,
Our counsel is hee clim;
But stay hee, or stray hee,
We have none help for him.

88   "Except the Cherrie be his chose,
Bee ye his friends, wee are his foes;
His doings we despite.
If we perceive him satled sa,
To satisfie him with the Slae,
His company we quite."
Then Dread and Danger grew so glad,
And wont that they had wun;
They thought all seald that they had said
Sen they had first begun;
They thought then, they mought then
Without a partie plead,
But yet there, with Wit there,
They were dung downe indeed.

blate timid   *chose* choice   *satled* settled
wont thought   *dung* knocked

89   "Sirs Dread and Danger," then quoth Wit,
"Ye did yourselves to mee submit;
Experience can prove."
"That," quoth Experience, "I past;
Their owne confession made them fast,
They may no more remove,
For if I right remember mee,
This maxime then they made,
To wit: the man with Wit should wey
What philosophs had said."
Which sentence, repentance,
Forbade him deare to buy.
They knew then, how true then,
And preasde not to reply.

90   Though hee dang Dread and Danger down,
Yet Courage could not overcome,
Hope heght him such an hyre;
He thought himselfe so soone he saw
His enemies were laid so law,
It was no time to tyre.
Hee hit the yron while it was hait,
Incace it might grow cold;
For he esteemde his foes defaite,
When once he found them folde.
"Though we now," quoth hee now,
"Have beene so free and franke,
Unsought yet, ye mought yet,
For kindnesse cund us thanke.

91   "Suppose it so as thou hast said,
That unrequyrde wee offered aide,
At least it came of love.
Experience, yee start too soone,
Yee dow nothing while all be done,
And then perhaps yee prove
More plaine than pleasant, too, perchance;
Some tell that have you tryit,

---

preasde not were not eager   *dang* knocked
heght promised   *hyre* reward   *hait* hot   *defaite* beaten
folde in retreat   *cund us thanke* expressed gratitude

As fast as you your selfe advance,
Ye dow not wel deny it.
Abide then, your tide then,
And waite upon the wind;
Ye know sir, ye ow sir,
To hold you ay behinde.

92   "When yee have done some doughty deeds,
Syne ye should see how all succeeds,
To write them as they were."
"Friend, huly, haste not halfe so fast,
Lest," quoth Experience, "at last,
Ye buy my doctrine deare.
Hope puts that haste into your head,
Which boyles your barmie braine.
Howbeit, fooles haste comes hulie speede,
Faire heights make fooles be faine.
Such smyling, beguiling,
Bids feare not for no freets;
Yet I now, deny now,
That al is gold that gleets.

93   "Suppose not silver all that shines,
Ofttimes a tentlesse merchant tines
For buying geare be gesse;
For all the vantage and the winning,
Good buyers gets at the beginning."
Quoth Courage, "Not the lesse,
Whiles as good merchant tines as wins,
If old mens tales bee true;
Suppose the pack come to [the] pins,
Who can his chance es[c]hew?
Then good sir, conclude sir,
Good buyers have done baith;
Advance then, take chance then,
As sundry good ships hath.

---

huly slowly   *barmie* frothy   *faine* glad   *freets* omens
gleets glitters   *tentlesse* careless   *the pack come to* [*the*] *pins* he wastes his wealth

94   "Who wist what would bee cheape or deare
Should neede to traffique but a yeare,
If things to come were kend.
Suppose all bygone things be plaine,
Your prophecy is but prophane,
Ye're best behold the end.
Yee would accuse mee of a crime
Almost before wee met.
Torment you not before the time,
Since dolour payes no debt.
What by past, that I past,
Ye wot if it was well;
To come yet, by doome yet,
Confesse ye have no feele."

95   "Yet," quoth Experience, "what than?
Who may be meetest for the man,
Let us his answere have."
When they submitted them to mee,
To Reason I was faine to flee,
His counsell for to crave.
Quoth he, "Since you yourselves submit
To doe as I decreet,
I shal advise with Skil and Wit,
What they thinke may bee meete."
They cryde then, "We byde then
At Reason for refuge;
Allow him, and trow him,
As governour and judge."

96   So said they all with one consent,
"What he concluds we are content,
His bidding to obey;
Hee hath authority to use;
Then take his chose whom he would chuse,
And longer not delay."
Then Reason rose and was rejoysde.
Quoth he, "Mine hearts, come hither;
I hope this play may bee composde,
That we may goe together.

---

doome judgment   *byde* submit (to)   *play* quarrel
composde resolved

To all now, I shall now
His proper place assigne.
That they heere shal say heere,
They thinke none other thing.

97   "Come on," quoth he, "companion Skill,
Ye understand both good and ill;
In physick yee are fine.
Be medciner unto this man
And shaw such cunning as yee can,
To put him out of paine.
First, gard the ground of all his griefe,
What sicknes ye suspect;
Syne looke what hee lackes for reliefe,
Ere further he infect.
Comfort him, exhort him,
Give him your good advice;
And panse not, nor skanse not,
The perill nor the price.

98   "Though it be cumbersome what recke?
Finde out the cause by the effect
And working of his veines.
Yet while we grip it to the ground,
See first what fashion may bee found
To pacifie his paines.
Doe what ye dow to have him haile
And for that purpose prease;
Cut off the cause, the effect must faile,
So all his sorrowes cease.
His fever shall never
From thencefoorth have no force;
Then urge him to purge him,
He will not waxe the worse."

---

physick medicine   *skanse* consider
what recke? what matter?   *haile* healthy   *prease* strive

99 Quoth Skil, "His senses are so sicke,
  I know no liquor worth a leeke
  To quench his deadly drouth;
  Except the Cherrie help his heat,
  Whose sappy sloking sharp and sweet,
  Might melt into his mouth
  And his melancholy remove,
  To mitigate his minde.
  None wholesomer for your behove,
  Nor more cooling of kinde;
  No nectar directar
  Could all the gods him give;
  Nor send him, to mend him,
  None like it, I believe,

100 "For drouth decayes as it digests."
  "Why then," quoth Reason, "nothing rests,
  But how it may bee had."
  "Most true," quoth Skil. "That is the scope,
  Yet we must have some helpe of Hope."
  Quoth Danger, "I am rad,
  His hastines breeds us mishap,
  When he is highly horst;
  I would wee looked ere wee lap."
  Quoth Wit, "That were not worst.
  I meane now, conveene now
  The counsell one and all;
  Begin then, cal on then."
  Quoth Reason, "So I shall."

101 Then Reason rose with gesture grave,
  Belyve conveening all the lave
  To see what they would say;
  With silver scepter in his hand,
  As chiftane chosen to command,
  And they bent to obey.

---

sappy sloking juicy quenching   *rad* advised   *belyve* immediately
lave rest

He pansed long before he spake
And in a study stood.
Syne hee began and silence brake:
"Come on," quoth he, "conclude,
What way now, we may now,
Yon Cherrie come to catch;
Speak out sirs, about sirs,
Have done, let us dispatch."

102   Quoth Courage, "Scourge him first that skars;
Much musing memory but marres."
"I tell you mine intent,"
Quoth Wit. "Who will not partly panse
In perils, perishes perchance,
Ou'r rackles may repent."
"Then," quoth Experience and spake,
"Sir, I have seene them baith,
In bairnlines and lye aback,
Escape and come to skaith.
But what now of that now?
Sturt followes all extreames.
Retaine then the meane then,
The surest way it seemes.

103   "Where some hes further'd, some hes faild,
Where part hes perisht, part prevaild,
Alike all cannot lucke.
Then either venture with the one,
Or, with the other, let alone
The Cherrie for to plucke."
Quoth Hope, "For feare folke must not fash."
Quoth Danger, "Let not light."
Quoth Wit, "Bee neither rude nor rash."
Quoth Reason, "Yee have right."
The rest then, though[t] best then,
When Reason said it so,
That roundly and soundly,
They should together goe,

pansed reflected   *skars* takes fright   *skaith* harm
sturt vexation   *lucke* be fortunate   *fash* be troubled

104   To get the Cherrie in all haste,
    As for my safety serving maist.
    Though Dread and Danger feard
    The peril of that irksome way,
    Lest that thereby I should decay,
    Who then so weake appearde,
    Yet Hope and Courage hard beside,
    Who with them wont contend,
    Did take in hand us for to guide
    Unto our journeyes end;
    Impleadging and waidging,
    Both two their lives for mine,
    Providing the guiding
    To them were granted syne.

105   Then Dread and Danger did appeale,
    Alledging it could not be well,
    Nor yet would they agree.
    But said they should sound their retreate
    Because they thought them no wise meete
    Conductores unto mee,
    Nor to no man in mine estate
    With sicknes sore opprest;
    For they tooke ay the nearest gate,
    Omitting oft the best.
    Their nearest perquearest
    Is always to them baith,
    Where they sir, may say sir,
    'What recks them of your skaith?'

106   "But as for us two, now we sweare
    By him before whom we appeare,
    Our ful intent is now
    To have you whole and alway was,
    That purpose for to bring to passe;
    So is not theirs I trow."

syne afterwards   *gate* way   *perquearest* fittest   *recks* matters
skaith harm

Then Hope and Courage did attest
The gods of both these parts,
If they wrought not all for the best
Of mee with upright hearts.
Our chiftane than liftane
His scepter, did enjoyne,
"No more there, uproare there!"
And so their strife was done.

107   Rebuiking Dread and Danger sore,
Suppose they meant well evermore
To me as they had sworne,
Because their neighbours they abusde,
In so farre as they had accusde
Them, as ye heard beforne.
"Did ye not else," quoth he, "consent
The Cherry for to pow?"
Quoth Danger, "We are well content,
But yet the maner how?
We shal now, even all now,
Get this man with us there.
It restis and best is,
Your counsel shall declare."

108   "Wel said," quoth Hope and Courage. "Now,
We thereto will accord with you
And shall abide by them;
Like as before we did submit,
So wee repeate the samine yit,
We minde not to reclaime.
Whom they shal chuse to guide the way,
Wee shal him follow straight,
And further this man what we may,
Because wee have so height.
Promitting, but flitting,
To doe the thing we can
To please both and ease both,
This silly sickly man."

attest call to witness   *pow* pull   *restis* remains
samine same   *reclaime* intend   *flitting* changing position

109   When Reason heard this, "Then," quoth hee,
"I see your chiefest stay to bee,
That we have nam'd no guide;
The worthy counsel hath, therefore,
Thought good that Wit should goe before,
For perils to provide."
Quoth Wit, "There is but one of three,
Which I shall to you show,
Whereof the first two cannot bee
For any thing I know.
The way heere so stay heere
Is, that wee cannot clim
Even ou'r now, we foure now;
That will bee hard for him.

110   "The next, if we goe downe about,
While that this bend of craiges run out,
The streame is there so starke
And also passeth wading deepe
And broader farre than we dow leape,
It should be idle wark.
It growes ay broader nere the sea,
Sen over the lin it came.
The running dead doth signifie
The deepnes of the same.
I leave now, to deave now,
How that it swiftly slides,
As sleeping and creeping,
But nature so provides.

111   "Our way then lyes about the lin,
Whereby a warrand we shal win,
It is so straight and plaine;
The water also is so shald,
We shal it passe even as we wald
With pleasure and but paine.
For as we see the mischief grow,
Oft of a feckles thing,

---

stay steep   *lin* waterfall   *deave* annoy with talk
shald shallow   *feckles* weak

So likewise doth this river flow
Foorth of a pretty spring;
Whose throat sir, I wot sir,
You may stop with your neive;
As you sir, I trow sir,
Experience, can prieve."

112   "That," quoth Experience, "I can.
All that yee said sen yee began,
I know to be of truth.
Quoth Skill, "The samine I approve."
Quoth Reason, "Then let us remove
And sleepe no more in sleuth.
Wit and Experience," quoth he,
"Shall come before apace;
The man shall come with Skill and mee
Into the second place.
Attour now, you foure now,
Shall come into a band;
Proceeding, and leading
Each other by the hand."

113   As Reason ordeinde all obeyde;
None was ou'r rash, nor none affraide –
Our counsel was so wise;
As of our journey Wit did note,
We found it true in every jote;
God bles'd our interprise.
For even as wee came to the tree,
Which, as yee heard mee tell,
Could not be clum, there suddenly
The fruite for ripenes fell.
Which hasting and tasting,
I found my selfe relievde
Of cares all and sares all,
Which minde and body grievde.

neive fist   *samine* same   *sleuth* sloth   *attour* moreover

114   Praise be to God, my Lord, therefore,
Who did mine health to mee restore,
Being so long time pinde.
Yea, blessed bee his holy Name,
Who did from death to life recleame
Mee, who was so unkinde.
All nations also magnifie
This everliving Lord.
Let me with you and you with mee,
To laude him ay accord.
Whose love ay wee prove ay
To us above all things;
And kisse him and blesse him,
Whose glore eternall rings.

Sweit Hairt rejoss in Mynd

1   Sweit hairt rejoss in mynd
With conforte day and nicht,
Ye have ane luif as kynd
As ever luifit weicht.
Thocht I be out of sicht
Latt nocht your courage fall,
My joyfull hert and licht
Ye haif and ever sal.

2   My bony burde be blyith
And ye sall find me so,
Imprent to you I kyith
To latt you nocht be woo.
Quhairever I ryde or go
Ye sall nocht sorie be,
My leill luif, hert and joo,
Nane hes my hairt bot ye.

3   And yie my trew luif sweit,
This do ye nocht gang stand,
My blyithnes for to beit
As I serve at your hand.

pinde tormented   *recleame* reclaim   *weicht* man   *licht* gay
burde girl   *imprent* constant   *kyith* declare   *woo* sad
leill luif faithful sweetheart   *gang stand,* oppose   *beit* overcome

To think me nocht constand
My bony burd lat be,
My constant hairt sal stand
To you quhill that I die.

4   I bid no mair of you
But god grant you his bliss;
God be als blyith of you
As I wald be of this,
Your lillie lippis to kiss,
Thinkand that mynd of youris,
My awin trew luif sche is
That luifis hir paramouris.

Quhill as with Whyt and Nimble Hand

1   Quhill as with whyt and nimble hand,
My maistres gathring flours doth stand
Amidst the florisht meid,
Of lilies whyt and violets,
A garland properly sho plets
To set upon hir heid.

2   O sun that shynis so bright above,
If ever thou the fyre of love
Hes felt as poets fayne –
If it be sik – as sik it semes,
Of courtessie withdraw thy bemes,
Leist thou hir colour stayne.

3   She, if thou not hir beutie burne,
Sall quyt thee with a better turne
To close hir cristall ees –
A brightnes far surmounting thyne,
Leist thou, thairby ashamd, suld tyne
Thy credit in the skyis.

---

quhill *that* until   *paramouris* lover
florisht meid flowery meadow   *sik* such   *quyt* repay
surmounting surpassing   *tyne* lose

A Description of Tyme

1   Tak tyme in tym or tym will not be tane –
Thairfor tak tent how thou this tyme suld tak.
Sho hes no hold to hold hir by bot ane,
A toppe befor bot beld behind hir bak.
Let thou hir slippe or slipperly grow slak,
Thou gettis no grippe agane fro sho be gane.
If thou wald speid, remember what I spak –
Tak tyme in tyme or tym will not be tane.

2   For I haif hard in adagies of auld
That tyme dois waist and weir all things away.
Then trow the taill that trew men oft hes tauld,
A turne in tyme is ay worth other tway.
Siklyk I haif hard oft-tymis suith men say
That negligence yit nevir furtherit nane.
Als seindle tymis luck folowes long delayis;
Tak tyme in tyme or tyme will not be tane.

Lyk as the Dum Solsequium

1   Lyk as the dum
Solsequium
With cair ou'rcum
And sorow when the sun goes out of sight
Hings doun his head
And droups as dead
And will not spread
Bot louks his leavis throu langour of the nicht,
Till folish Phaeton ryse
With whip in hand
To cleir the cristall skyis
And light the land,
Birds in thair bour
Luiks for that hour
And to thair prince ane glaid good-morow givis,
Fra thyn that flour
List not to lour
Bot laughis on Phoebus lousing out his leivis.

tent care   *toppe* forelock   *beld* bald   *seindle tymis* seldom   *dum* silent
solsequium marigold   *louks* locks up   *list* desires   *lour* mourn

2   So fairis with me
       Except I be
       Whair I may se
       My lamp of licht my Lady and my Love.
       Fra sho depairts
       Ten thousand dairts
       In syndrie airts
       Thirlis throu my hevy hart but rest or rove.
       My countenance declairs
       My inward grief,
       Good hope almaist dispairs
       To find relief.
       I die, I dwyn,
       Play does me pyn –
       I loth on eviry thing I look – alace,
       Till Titan myne
       Upon me shyne,
       That I revive throu favour of hir face.

3   Fra she appeir
       [Into hir spheir]
       Begins to cleir
       The dawing of my long desyrit day.
       Then Curage cryis
       On Hope to ryse
       Fra he espyis
       My noysome nicht of absence worne away.
       No wo when I awalk
       May me impesh
       Bot on my staitly stalk
       I florish fresh.
       I spring, I sprout,
       My leivis ly out –
       My color changes in ane hartsum hew.
       No more I lout
       Bot stands up stout
       As glade of hir for whom I only grew.

airts places   *thirlis* pierces   *rove* repose   *dwyn* dwindle
loth on detest   *dawing* dawning   *impesh* prevent
hartsum pleasant   *lout* bow down

4   O happie day
   Go not away,
   Apollo stay
   Thy chair from going doun into the West,
   Of me thou mak
   Thy zodiak
   That I may tak
   My plesur to behold whom I love best.
   Thy presence me restores
   To lyf from de[ath],
   Thy absence also shores
   To cut my brea[th].
   I wish in vane
   Thee to remane
   Sen 'primum mobile' sayis alwayis nay;
   At leist thy wane
   Turn soon agane,
   [Fareweill with patience perforce till day.]

Away, Vane World

1   Away vane world, bewitcher of my hairt!
   My sorowis shawis, my sins maks me to smart!
     Yit will I not dispair
     Bot to my God repair –
      He hes mercy ay,
      Thairfor will I pray.
   He hes mercy ay and lovis me
   Thoght by his humbling hand he provis m[e].

2   Away, away, too long thou hes me snaird!
   I will not tyne more tyme, I am prepaird
     Thy subtill slychts to flie,
     Whilks hes allured me.
      Tho they sweitly smyle,
      Smoothly they begyle:
   Tho they sweitly smyle, I feir thame.
   I find thame fals, I will forbeir thame.

chair chariot *shores* threatens *sen* since *provis* tests
tyne lose   *slychts* wiles

3   Once more away, shawis loth the world to lea[ve],
    Bids oft adeu with it that holds me slave.
     Loth am I to forgo
     This sweet alluring fo.
      Sen thy wayis ar vane,
      Sall I the retane?
    Sen thy wayis ar vane, I quyt thee.
    Thy plesuris sall no more delyt me.

4   A thousand tymis away! Oh, stay no more!
    Sweit Chryst conduct, leist subtile sin devore!
     Without thy helping hand
     No man hes strenth to stand.
      Tho I oft intend
      All my wayis to mend,
    Tho I oft intend, strength fails ay.
    The sair assaults of sin prevailis ay.

5   Quhat sal I say? Ar all my plesurs past?
    Sall worldly lustis now tak thair leiv at last?
     Yea, Chryst, these earthly toyes
     Sall turne in hevinly joyes.
      Let the world be gone,
      I'l love Chryst allone!
    Let the world be gone – I cair not.
    Chryst is my love alone – I feir not.

Hay, now the Day Dawis

1   Hay, now the day dawis,
    The jolie cok crawis,
    Now shroudis the shawis
     Throu Natur anone.
    The thissell-cok cryis
    On lovers wha lyis
    Now skaillis the skyis,
     The nicht is neir gone.

---

shawis shows   *shawis* groves   *anone* at once
thissell-cok male mistle-thrush *skaillis* clears

2 The feilds ou'rflowis
    With gowans that growis
    Quhair lilies lyk low-is
     Als rid as the rone.
    The turtill that trew is
    With nots that renewis
    Hir pairtie persewis,
     The night is neir gone.

3 Now hairtis with hyndis
    Conforme to thair kyndis
    Hie tursis their tyndis
     On grund whair they grone.
    Now hurchonis with hairis
    Ay passis in pairis,
    Quhilk deuly declaris,
     The night is neir gone.

4 The sesone excellis
    Thrugh sweetnes that smellis
    Now Cupid compellis
     Our hairtis echone
    On Venus wha waikis
    To muse on our maikis
    Syn sing for thair saikis,
     The night is neir gone.

5 All curageous knichtis
    Aganis the day dichtis
    The breist plate that bright is
     To feght with thair fone.
    The stoned steed stampis
    Throu curage and crampis
    Syn on the land lampis,
     The night is neir gone.

---

low-is flames *rone* rowan berry
pairtie mate *tursis* tosses *tyndis* antlers
hurchonis hedgehogs *echone* each one *maikis* mates
dichtis prepare *crampis* swaggers *lampis* strides along

D   97

6 The freikis on feildis
   That wight wapins weildis
   With shyning bright shieldis
    At Titan in trone,
   Stiff speiris in reistis
   Ouer cursoris cristis
   Ar brok on thair breistis,
    The night is neir gone.

7 So hard ar their hittis
   Some sweyis, some sittis
   And some perforce flittis
    On grund whill they grone.
   Syn groomis that gay is
   On blonkis that brayis
   With swordis assayis,
    The night is neir gone.

freikis soldiers *wapins* weapons
reistis rests (for a lance or spear) *cursoris* war horses
cristis plumes *flittis* die *blonkis* steeds

John Stewart of Baldynneis

Roland Furious – The 11 Cant

Perplexit pen againe to paine apply!
Denunce the teirs that from thy dyt distels!
Now for your ayde Ramnusia I cry
To reule arycht the rancor intermels.
This trublous teine my tyrit toung compels   5
To dry for drouth that I may not declair,
Within this goulf quhair source of sorrow swels
My sensis so suffuscat ar with cair.
Wold god, Bocace mycht in my place repair
This tragedie perfytlie to compyle;   10
Or reverent Ovid wold the sammyng spair
In metamorphois of his steitlie style.
For lyk as myrth dois mak the visage smyle
Or plesand lycht rejosis moir the ie
Than deip perbrouilyeit dungeons dark and vyle,   15
So wanton verse moir aptlie dois aggrie
To pouse the pithles spreit with sum supplie,
Quhilk I posses, laiking the curius vaine,
Than mirthles mateirs that amazis me
And doubill duls my dolorus dullit braine.   20
Yit sen the burding dois on me remaine
To sport my Prence, quhois courtasie bening
May mak me aide, as meed the gowldin graine,
Quhilk did Eneas to his journay bring,
I indevoir the remanent to sing   25
Of Rolands fall in furie at the last.
Help at this neid O greizlie ghests maling
With spedie pen to mak this propose past.
Compact in breiff this bailfull bittir blast,
Quhilk dois my style renverse in disaray   30
And all my sensis na les maks agast
Than Nabuchodonosors great decay.

dyt writing	*distels* fall	*intermels* mingles	*teine* vexation
suffuscat suffocated	*sammyng* same	*perbrouilyeit* parboiled	
pouse push along	*curius* melancholy	*burding* burden	
bening benign	*meed* did	*graine* bough	*indevoir* endeavour
furie madness	*greizlie* grisly	*maling* baleful	*propose* subject
renverse overturn			

The monarck Ninus that in preson lay
Of croune bereft and captive to the deed,
The puissant Cyrus, King of Perse, I say,　　　　35
Quho vincust Cresus syn did lose his heed,
Great Alexander poysand but remeed,
Nor mychtie Cesar, quho was schortlie slaine,
Skairse represents so lairge of fortouns feed,
As our Comte Roland quho did lose his braine.　　40
O frivole fortoune, fikile, false and vaine
Quhy dois thou vex this world with sic annoy?
Thou hich exalts, law to deject againe;
Thy quheile ay tumbling with decetfull toy.
All that suppons maist suirlie till injoy　　　　45
Thy hautie wavering hairis with the wind,
With subtile smyle oft tyms thou dois distroy
And for reward presents thy pow behind.
No force avails thy fikilnes to bind.
Dame Indiscreit I sute of the no grace;　　　　50
Thou art my fo, for I culd nevir find
No kynd of favor in thy fenyeit face.
His majestie hes power in this cace
With sweit regarde thy sournes till assuadge,
Quhois royale feit maist humylie I imbrace　　　55
To saif me from thy rancor and thy radge.
Thy course inconstant in till everie adge
Pruife dois recorde, thocht I not specefie.
Great Bajacet that Turk thou did incadge
Quhom Tamberlan maist duilfullie meed drie　　60
Ane extreme slavrie till that he did die;
The one thou did from bass estait avance
And dang the uther doune from hich degrie,
So is the coustume of thy fatall chance.
For to record that potent King of France,　　　65
Quho in the sporting of his manlie spreit
Unto the deed was percit with ane lance,
Is pruife that thou in variance dois fleit.
King Alexander is exemple meit,
Quho reuld above the antique Scottis keine;　　70
The hardie force quhairwith he was repleit,

---

vincust conquered　　　*remeed* cure　　　*feed* enmity
quheile wheel　　　*toy* bauble　　*pow* bald head　　*fenyeit* deceitful
humylie humbly　　*dang* beat　　*fleit* change ground　　*meit* fitting
keine bold

Nor yit the prudence quhilk did in him scheine,
Could not eschew the rigor of thy teine
Bot creuallie be the he was forlorn
In picking of his horse as mycht be seine   75
Above the rock thair situat at Kingorn.
For as the rose annexit to the thorn,
So is thy plesour with sum paine prepaird;
Or as the wyde increscis with the corn,
So thou perturbs the cheifest but regaird.   80
Quho walks at will within thy wavering yaird
And dois delyt to smell thy suggurit gall,
With suddan storm his stait sall not be spaird
Bot as Pompey or hardie Hanniball,
So sall occur in fin thair fatale fall.   85
The strong, redouttit, dochtie Darius,
Quho lang did dant his mychtie nychtbours all
Be venim of thy visage varius,
Quhan force of fois he fand contrarius,
New battell thryse he bauldlie did conveine   90
Bot ruittit out he was as Arius.
First did he lose his kingdome and his queine,
His mother, guids and childrine all was seine
In the possession of his enemie;
Syn lost his lyf and mycht na wayis obteine   95
At his last breath so meikile laser frie
As native freind or serviteur to sie,
Bot in his chariot wondit to the deed
He thocht it did his painfull spreit supplie,
Quhan till his fo his last regrait he meed.   100
Queine Semerame thou lang did welthie leed,
Quha in hir courage disaguisde hir kynd
Bot all thy favor turnit in to feed
At hir last battell with the King of Ynd.
Dame Panthasile, quhais hich magnanime mynd   105
Did thrall the boldnes of the Grecians stout,
Thocht for ane space thou prosperus inclynd
With blast of fame to sound hir praisis out,
In tragedie alwayis thou brocht about
Hir proud attempt and mychtie mundan gloir;   110

---

teine rage   *wyde* weed   *suggurit* sugared
dochtie doughty   *bauldlie* boldly   *conveine* assemble   *laser* leisure
feed enmity   *mundan* worldly

Scho and hir ladies all that seimlie rout
Did vincust die, quhilk dewlie I deploir.
Zenobia, quham beuteis did decoir,
Hir profund prudence nor hir hardie hand
Mycht not resist thy malice onie moir   115
Fra ans scho did Aurelius gainstand,
Quho brocht hir captiv from hir native land
And till triumphe above this cairfull queine
His persone fixit at ane chariot band
And drew hir so throch Rome apertlie seine.   120
O crewall fortoune, noysum was thy teine;
Thocht scho presumd all Asia to gyd,
Thy recompance maist freuch and frivole beine;
So all are served that dois in the confyd.
Thy slipprie solas dois al schortlie slyd   125
As yse dissolves with flam of fervent fyre:
Thy douce delyt with dolor is devyd,
Quhan we belive to find our harts desyre:
With fikile fassone so thou dois impyre,
Quhill everie stait my sie the facill flot: 130
Thou gifs no gaine to him quho merits hyre
Bot at thy lust dois attribute the lot:
Thou maks the giltie sum tyme seime but spot
And guid desert in to the dust dings doune:
Wit walkith oft in till ane raggit cot   135
And folie set up in ane velvet goune:
Ane laird be the becums ane meschant lowne,
Ane lowne againe be the is meed ane laird,
So in all things thou art ay blindlie bowne
To rycht nor resone haifing no regaird.   140
Thou rakles rins as rasche and restles baird,
Both up and doune, befoir and now abak;
I knaw no puissant, erdlie pomp prepaird
Thy frivole frailnes firmlie to coak.
Gif ether wisdome, force or wordie fak   145
Mycht haif rebellit quhaire thy baile is boune,
Than Roland haid be the susteind na lak
Bot evir hichlie borne the palmie croune,

---

vincust vanquished   *apertlie* openly
noysum harmful   *teine* rage   *freuch* brittle   *impyre* rule
facill flot easily floating   *raggit cot* ragged coat
meschant lowne worthless servant   *baird* minstrel   *coak* coerce
wordie fak worthy deed

Quhom thy deceit degressis na les doune
Nor Hector, traillit at Achylles steid,   150
Was changeit from that Hector of renoune,
Quho umquhyle reft Achylles of his weid.
Impolist pen to propose new proceid,
Returne to text and dyt of Roland rycht.
He most induir and I most schaw indeid   155
This alteration quhilk did on him lycht.
Now eftir that this strong redouttit knycht
Be ampill pruife all uthers did precell,
Quhill all the world abaisit of his mycht,
At last in schersing Mandricard so fell   160
He seis ane christall revere douce distell
About the bordour of ane mydow fair,
Quhair flouris fresche maist savoruslie did smell
And monie seimlie frondise trie preclair
Obumbrat all this situation rair.   165
Doune he descends amyds the blossoms greine
For to refresche him in the temperat air,
Sen dayis two he haid in travell beine
In sutting of the foirsaid Sarraseine.
Bot heir depryvit was he of repois   170
And all his confort turnit in to teine,
Quhan that his wofull eine haid done disclois
The vive handwreting of his onlie chois,
Ingravit thair on monie growand graine;
For this was even the veirray place formois,   175
Quhair scho and Medor wont was to remaine.
In thousand wayis that part did all explaine
Thair schyphert nams, as I haif schawne befoir,
Bot everie lettir bruist his bailfull braine
And percit throch his wondit hart als soir   180
As duilfull deedlie dart him to devoir.
With monie wayis maist cairfullie he socht
Till schift the sorrow that so did him schoir
And not to credit sic ane noysum thocht,
Efforcing him with feirfull spreit afflocht   185
For to belive that scho of hir guid grace

---

umquhyle formerly   *weid* clothing   *propose* purpose   *precell* surpass
fell fierce   *frondise* leafy   *preclair* very bright   *obumbrat* shaded
sutting following   *vive* clear   *onlie chois* chosen one   *graine* branches
formois beautiful   *schyphert* monogrammed   *devoir* devour
schoir threaten   *afflocht* distressed

In his remembrance haid thois wordis wrocht,
Him so surnaming Medor in this place;
Or that sum uther Angelique percace,
So in this sort haid done thair luif furthschaw.   190
Bot full assuirit was he yit alace
For the characters suirlie did he knaw,
Quhilk his awne ladie usit ay to draw;
Bot could nawayis him self belive at all.
So with opinions he the treuth did thraw,   195
As doutfull trust did in his fancie fall
Him self to suadge with sum assurance small.
Bot as hote collis with sum wattir cold
First seims to slaik, yit eftirwart thay sall
Upblais in fyre more ferventlie and bold,   200
Even so the moir that he extinguise wold
His glowing greif, the sam the moir did ryis.
As feltert foule, quhilk glew or girn dois hold,
The moir scho flychters scho the faster lyis,
The moir also that he did deip devyis   205
This mortall pansive terror till eschew,
The moir profound his paine did him suppryis,
Quhilk force nor wisdom mycht nawayis reskew.
In this estate approtching neir he drew
Till the caverne above ane fontane cleir,   210
Quhair wodbind and vyn brainchis linkit threw
Ane plesand tortur at the entress heir,
Decoring all this proper part so deir
To both the foirsaid luifers everie day;
For quhan fair Phebus with his heit seveir   215
Did brymlie byrne, heirin imbrast thay lay;
Quhairfoir thair nams both in and out I say
Heir drawne was ofter than in onie place;
With cake, with coll and pensile scharp alway,
Both heir and thair was schawne thair happie cace.   220
The cairfull comte with sad dejectit face
Ful monie luiflie dictums heir did vew
Be Medor wrocht, quhilks at the sammyng space
Als recent fair and vivelie formit schew
As instantlie thay haid beine forgit new.   225

surnaming nicknaming   *percace* perchance
furthschaw broadcast   *thraw* contest   *suadge* appease   *feltert* entangled
glew birdlime   *girn* snare   *flychters* flutters   *wodbind* woodbine
cake chalk   *coll* charcoal   *cace* situation

And for the fervent wonderfull delyt
That heir did to this Adonis insew,
In verse he drew this subsequent indyt,
Quhilk wretin was maist plainlie and perfyt
In his awne langage, as I do suppois,   230
Quhairof the sentence I sall heir recyt,
Thocht I exactlie may it not disclois.
   O herbis greine and prettie plants formois,
   O limpid wattir springing suave and cleir,
   O cave obscuir aggriabill to thois   235
   Quho wold tham cuile in thy fresche umber deir,
   Quhair Angelique maist beutifull but peir
   In vaine desyrd be uthers monie mo,
   Oft nakit lay betwix my armes heir.
   I, Medor puir, quhom ye haif eisit so   240
   May not requyt you moir, bot quhair I go
   Your praise sall evir stedfastlie induir.
   Lords, ladies, knychts and lustie luifers tho
   And everie gentle hart I will procuir
   To wiss you weill and frie of dainger suir.   245
   Both sone and mone and nymphs you saif from tort
   And nevir pastor with his troup injuir
   Your verduir ritche, O seimlie fair resort.
     Bot ay about you birdis blythlie sing
     And unmolestit be your silver spring.   250
In toung Arabic wretin was this thing,
Quhilk langage Roland rycht expertlie knew
And oft he red it contrarie to wring
The veirray sentence from the mening trew.
Bot ay the moir that he did so persew,   255
Moir plaine and ampill did the text appeir,
Quhilk to the death his thirlit hart neir threw.
Assault of sorrow socht him so seveir,
That staring still he stuid astonist heir
For wo almaist void of his wittis all,   260
With havie fixit eis and cairfull cheir
Upon the stone as sensles stonie wall;
His chin declyning on his brest did fall
And cloud of cair held doune his cumlie front,

indyt poem
formois beautiful   *suave* pleasant   *cuile* cool   *umber* shade
but peir peerless   *puir* poor   *tort* wrong   *ampill* complete
thirlit enslaved   *socht* attacked   *front* brow

Quhair left was no audacitie to brall   265
For boyling baile his boudin braine haid blont.
Great egar greif so grivous did surmont,
That he onnawayis mycht relasche his wo
With wofull words as umquhyle he was wont,
Nor yit no teiris from his eine could go,   270
His liquid humor suffocat was so
As quhan in veschell wyd with narrow throt
The wattir choks and may not flow thairfro
For great aboundance that dois in it flot.
No wonder now althocht his brest be blot   275
With dainger deip of deedlie duill in deid,
Bot yit his hoip could not dissolve the knot
Quhilk in his ladies loyaltie did breid.
So with sum trust betosd and meikill dreid
He scherst his thochts to think this thocht untrew   280
(Quhairon his fancie for ane space did feid)
And ferventlie dois wiss it till insew,
That sum evilwiller all thois dictums drew
For to diffame his constant ladie frie,
And be sic bittir blame his baile to brew,   285
That suddanlie quhan he the sam suld sie
For percing paine mycht at that instant die.
"O lord," sayis he, "quhat vehement dispyt
Hes he declaird, quhom evir so it be.
Weill imitat hes he hir hand perfyt   290
In drawing of this nochtie noysum dyt."
So with this feibile esperance at last
Sum thing assuagit was his former fyt,
And thus againe on Bridedor he past.
The day declynd and nycht approtchit fast;   295
Fair Tytans steids haid rune thair utter race,
Quhois giltit hairs disparpling bak did cast
Throche asurit sky quhilk elss obscuird his face,
Till his palle sister Phebe giffing place,
Quhan that the pynit Paladeine did tend   300
His course, na les incertaine at this space
Than schip but rudder quhilk dois wilsum wend.

---

brall soar
boudin bold   *blont* blunted   *umquhyle* formerly   *suffocat* stifled
blot stained   *hoip* hope   *did breid* originated   *betosd* tossed around
diffame discredit   *frie* noble   *nochtie* evil   *noysum* harmful
fyt fit   *disparpling* scattering   *wilsum* wilfully

Bot yit, or he his voyage far did spend,
From tops of houssis till him did appeir
The smok of fyrie vapeur up ascend.   305
Bald barking doggis also did he heir
And monie flokis making meikill beir,
Sum routting loud and sum did semplie blait.
Unto the village quhan the compt cam neir,
He lychtit doune because it was so lait,   310
Quhair radelie ane boy discreit and fait
Did tak the gydment of his horse in cuir.
Sum did desarme his person of estait,
Sum loust the giltit spurris quhilk he buir
And sum attending stuid upon the fluir   315
For till obey as plesit him command.
Now this was even the verray ludging suir,
Quhair wondit Medor all his weilfair fand.
The stressit knycht all stupefact did stand
And wold to bed but onie kynd of fuid;   320
Sic gripping greif about his bosom band
That appetyt from meit was far excluid.
For fillit full of havie rancor ruid,
He did behold with goustlie visage palle
The wofull wreat, quhilk frizit up his bluid;   325
Depaint on posts and windocks of the hall,
On durs, on tabils and on everie wall,
Both Angelique and Medor schyphert beine
With luiflie knottis interlasit small,
In thousand sorts apertlie to be seine.   330
The trublit comte could not abstract his eine
From sycht of that quhilk wrocht him greattest paine,
And tending oft to crave quhat it sould meine,
Feir for to find his feirfull thocht meed plaine
Caust him againe his lippis close restraine.   335
So from him self he wold the treuth oscuir
With trimbling dreid in his perturbit braine
Sum suadgement schersing be consait unsuir.
Bot crewall fortone at sic feid him buir,
That scho no paine wold from his persone spair   340
But tuik delyt this chiftan till injuir,

beir noise   *blait* bleat   *radelie* eagerly   *fait* smart
did tak the gydment of his horse in cuir cared for the management of his horse
loust loosened   *wreat* writing   *frizit* freezed   *depaint* depicted
windocks windows   *apertlie* openly   *consait unsuir* unlikely fancy
at sic feid him buir was so much his foe

His musing mynd mischiving mair and mair.
No thing avalit his obfuscat cair
With cloud of dout quhairin he held his pace,
For ane at lenth did all the trewth declair   345
But inquisition of this cairfull cace;
Quhilk was the pastor, quho in to that place
Be broikin sychis did persave his wo,
And till appaise his pansive spreit ane space
Began the histoir of the luifers two –   350
First quhow that Medor, deedlie wondit so,
He thair did bring at Angeliques desyre,
Quha cuird his hurt; than quhow that scho did go
For him consuming all in luifis fyre
Swa that of honor thochtles or impyre   355
Scho to this sempill souldart did inclyn,
And band up mariage for to quenche desyre.
Thus he the histoir rycht in everie lyn
Did so discus quhill that hir braslat fyn
He representit at that instant steed.   360
This was the ax at last descendan syn
With deedlie dint quhilk did ding of his heed.
Lang speitchles lay he strukin almaist deed,
Quhill source of sorrow mycht no moir susteine,
Bot furiuslie outbirstit but remeed   365
Sobs from his mouth and teiris from his eine.
Bot most of all quhan solitar he beine
Ane fluid aboundant bouting out besprent
His boudin brest all swellit up in teine,
And both his cheaks bebathing but relent   370
Deip in him now was cauld dispair imprent,
Yit from his birnand bosome fast did flow
Hote flammyng sychs quhilk nevir could be spent;
So fell and fervent was the fyrie low,
Quhilk in his hart ay moir and moir did grow   375
But onie slaiking thocht it fumit out;
His breath bot onlie did as belleis blow

mischiving harming	*avalit* assisted (in lessening)		*obfuscat* gloomy
pastor shepherd	*pansive* reflective	*impyre* power	*souldart* soldier
braslat bracelet	*syn* then	*dint* blow	*did ding* struck
bouting springing	*besprent* besprinkled	*boudin* bold	*low* flame
belleis bellows			

To kendle all his bodie round about,
And als his eine did serve bot for ane spout
The vitale humeur from his lyf to draw, 380
For sorrow suir not cled with former dout
Did all his arters vive aschunder thraw.
Quho may the strese intolerabile schaw,
Quhilk did this valyant warior so torne?
Leile, lychtleit luifers onlie may it knaw, 385
Quho haples fruite of jelousie hes schorne.
In bed he restles tumblit thus forlorne,
Quhilk did moir dour than dourest stone appeir;
Ilk softest fedder was as poyntit thorne
To prick his persone or the scharpest breir. 390
The walkryf thochtis of his cair seveir
Permits him nocht to sleip ane moment space.
Turne as he wold both hither, thair and heir,
Raidge of his rancor did him ay imbrace
And in this torment he bethocht, alace, 395
That his unkyndlie, darrest ladie quhyt
Haid interteind hir Medor in this place;
Heirfoir the sammyng (plinist with dispyt)
He did abhorre and from it bendit quyt.
As quhan ane pastor schersing eisment lyis 400
Amongs the tender flouris of delyt,
Syn at his feit ane yssing serpent spyis
Maist quyklie and astonist up till ryis,
So Roland full of dolor and desdaine
With diligence for all his harneis cryis 405
And in that ludgeing wold no moir remaine,
Bot montit on his Bridedor againe
And wold not tarie quhill Aurora brycht
Haid spred hir silver schaddow on the plaine,
Bot throch the feilds ryds all this vilsum nycht. 410
He plains, he pains and as ane furious wycht
Blasphems the heavens, the stars and gods devyn,
With trickling teirs beblubring all his sycht
And syching insatiantlie for pyn.
Yea, thocht the morrow cleir arryvit syn 415
But intervall his sorrow did induir.

---

humeur bodily humour   *leile* faithful   *lychtleit* disdained
walkryf wakeful   *schersing* searching   *yssing* hissing   *harneis* armour
vilsum evil   *beblubring* obscuring   *sycht* vision
but intervall ceaselessly

From brochs and citeis far he did declyn,
Eschewing sycht of everie creatuir,
To dern deserts and partis maist obscuir
With wofull vult he wandrit all the day   420
But onie knawleidge quhair his horse him buir;
And with maist grivous great regraitting ay
Did fill the heaven, the air and feilds alway.
He fround for furie, feilling in his heed
The storms of raidge pelmell about fast play.   425
In winter bald Neptunus nevir meed
Moir motion fell in fomie fluidis reed,
As tumults strong tormoyling to and fro
Of braying baile quhilk in his brest abeed,
With trublit tempest him tormenting so.   430
Than in the nycht quhan all to rest did go
He doune discendit in ane bocage greine,
With cairfull skrychis evir waltring tho
And sic scharp schours of sorrow did susteine
That sleip mycht nevir close his weping eine,   435
Quhairfra ten thousand teiris did distell,
As quhan from bourn that lang hes dammit beine
Streams breaks aboundant quhilk thairin did swell.
Him self astonit could not think nor tell
Quhow possibill so monie teiris mycht   440
Poure from his eis, quhilks lyk ane springing well
Did nevir stay thair rynning day nor nycht.
Than syching soir he said, "This liquor brycht
Is no moir teirs. Teirs may not end my wo,
Quhilk bot begins. And spent ar from my sycht   445
My teirs all. This source quhilk springis so
I knaw it is vive vapor fleing fro
The fervent flams, quhilk birns my hart to deed
Up throch my soddin brest, syn out dois go
At my two eis and sall draw but remeed   450
My lyf and dolor both at ons to feed;
Bot sen so is, sched out thy course with speid
And my unhappie dayis to end soon leed,
And ye O sychs quhairwith my cair dois feid,
Ye are no sychs; sychs may not ay proceid   455
But onie cease as thois that I exspyre.

brochs burghs	*dern* secret	*vult* countenance
great lament	*bocage* grove	*skrychis* screams *waltring* tottering on
bourn brook	*but remeed* without cure	

The moir I sych, moir panting breath dois breid.
The lord of luife, quho birns me all in fyre,
Maks with his wings this wind and will not tyre
To cause my kendlit flammes evir flow   460
Quhill I destroyit be both bon and lyre.
Bot O great mervell, that my hart now dow
So long induir in luifis fervent low
And unconsumit utterlie to nocht!
Bot quhom am I in quhom sic raidge dois grow?   465
Am I that Roland quho hes wonders wrocht?
No. Roland treulie in his grafe is brocht;
His dame ingrait hes wranguslie him slaine.
I am bot onlie his puir spreit afflocht
In wildernese heir forcit to complaine   470
My desperat, maist great infernale paine;
To beir record be my profoundest wo
Quhat everie ane may hoip for till attaine,
Quho thrallit in the links of luife dois go."
This nycht till end Roland lamentit so   475
And quhan the vermell matutina sched
In celest hews hir adgeit husband fro,
Him leving sleipand in his donckie bed,
And quhan the worldis lycht began to spred
Brycht rubie sparkis throch the purpur sky,   480
Be destenie the comte haid so beine led
That in the part he him persavit ly
Besyd the rock, quhilk he befoir did spy
With Angelique and Medor gravit all,
For force of furie than his flesche did fry.   485
Be dints and stogs of dochtie Durandal
The craig and wreat he claive in skelpis small.
So dois he go hich radgeing in dispyt
And suddanlie to ground renversit all,
Quhair onie trait was of the luiflie dyt.   490
The savage pastor and his troup may quyt
Cauld cumlie umbrage of this cave for ay
And that fair fontan, springand silver quhyt
With restles rumor throch the sprutand spray.

---

kendlit kindled
bon and lyre flesh and bone   *ingrait* ungrateful   *afflocht* afflicted
vermell matutina rosy morning   *donckie* dampish   *dints* strokes
stogs thrusts   *wreat* writing   *skelpis* splinters   *renversit* overthrew
trait trace   *quyt* do without   *rumor* murmur   *sprutand* growing

Thocht recent liquor clarifeit alway,   495
It spoutit out as colorit christall cleine,
Yit could the same in nothing quenche I say
The coler fell quhilk in him birnand beine.
Great stoks and stons and monie brainchis greine
Thairin he swackit and did nevir spair,   500
Quhill all that wattir cleir as saphir scheine
Was drumlie trublit in ilk conduict clair.
Than irkit full of swet and havie cair
But poust he breathles on the mydow fell
In sorrow sowpit syching sad and sair,   505
Concluding heir continewallie to dwell.
No heit, no cauld, no raine nor windis snell
Mycht mak him ons to leif againe this place,
Quhairin he lay (as dois the histoir tell)
But speitche and evir with affixit face   510
The firmament beholding all the space;
And so but meet or drink did still induir,
Quhill that the dririe nycht haid rune hir race
Thryse cled in till hir clouddie robbe obscuir,
And quhill Apollo thryse haid montit suir   515
In gouldin cart to luminat the day.
And grevous rigor quhilk his.bodie buir
In feibling him it moir agmentit ay,
Quhill at the last all vincust quhair he lay,
Be paine heirof out of his sens he start   520
And all his judgement from him fled away.
Than the fourt day working his proper smart
His hands outragius did his visage skart
Maist horribile and with ane hiddeus brall
For raidge he roird and restles did dispart   525
His scheild, his gantlat and his corslat tall.
Heir fell the brassats, thair lyis Durandal,
Strong nails he breaks, his cuissots aff did slyd,
His helm, his gorget and his harneis all
In thousand peicis he disparplit wyd.   530

swackit struck	*drumlie* gloomily	*conduict* conduit	*poust* strength
sowpit supped	*snell* bitter	*obscuir* dark	*skart* tear	*brall* noise
dispart cleave	*brassats* arm-pieces	*cuissots* thigh-pieces	
harneis armour	*disparplit* scattered		

Ay moir and moir his furie did hym gyd
From hour till hour, quhill it increscit so
That in no part he permanent wold byd,
Bot ravand wodlie swift and rasche did go.
His clothing all and sark he reft him fro   535
And nakit schew his wombe, his brest and bak.
With flyring face his mouth did morgeon tho
And syndrie sounds maist terribile did mak,
Ay claverand loud and not to propose spak.
Syn quhan his raidge wold reull him moir seveir,   540
He at ane pull wold suddanlie uptak
The greatest oike or fir that he cam neir
As bled of buss or berrie aff the breir.
Great rocks, caverns and montans all about
He meed resound, and with ane luik austeir   545
Abaist the pastors, chaceand everie rout
That for to spy his folie ischit out;
And quhair he cam but mercie or remeed
Uprais amongs tham ane maist feirfull schout.
Sum with his fist lay fellit in that steed,   550
Sum dammest doune, sum bruisit to the deed,
Sum gat thair brest quyt broikin or thair bak,
Fra sum he puld the arme, the leg or heed;
Syn in his hand the bluidie boulk wold tak
And at ane uther egarlie it swak.   555
Tham ranging thus with ronklit front upbend
He meed great heaps of this unhappie pak
And nane of all agains him durst pretend.
For as the weyld and furius ours dois stend
But onie feir or sussie for to sie,   560
The Russians hunters tym and travell spend
For to persew hir throche the montans hie;
Thocht than approtche hir ane great cumpanie
Of little hounds, quhowsoon scho blinks about,
That feibile sort all skattrit bak dois flie;   565
Even so, quhan raging Roland ruschit out,

---

wodlie madly   *flyring* mocking
morgeon grimace   *claverand* drivelling   *to propose* pertinently
oike oak   *bled* piece   *buss* bush   *abaist* cowed   *ischit* sortied
dammest doune knocked senseless   *boulk* implement   *swak* brandish
ours bear   *sussie* trouble

The peuple all fast fled in deedlie dout
With all the speid and diligence thay mycht
And so dissoverit was this rakless rout,
Sum closit tham in ludgeings strong and wycht,   570
Sum montit up on tours or templs hicht
And sum low spying under covert lay
Of this maist sensles fole till haif ane sycht,
Quho on the feilds dismembrit everie day
Bauld buls and beufils in his sport and play.   575
He raifs, he rugs, he bruisis, breaks and ryfs
With hands, with feit, with nails and teith alway;
He byts, he stricks, he tumbls, he turns, he stryfs,
He glaiks, he gaips, he girns, he glours, he dryfs
Throw moss and montane, forrest, firth and plaine,   580
The birds, the beists, the boyes, the men and wyfs
With bruit moir hiddeus from his trublit braine
Than force of fluidis hurlland in great raine.
Foull glar and dust his face all filthie meed,
Quhairin no former beutie did remaine   585
And both his eis for wraith was boudin reed,
Quhilks up and doune ay turnit in his heed
With fearce regard upcasting all the quhyt.
Both nycht and day he in the feilds abeed
And for to fill his houngrie appetyt   590
Fuid quhair he mycht he reft with great dispyt.
Swyft harts and hynds he also wold devoir
And to the death in rageing furie smyt
The sangler strong, the tygar or the boir
And tham in gobbats gredelie all toir,   595
Thair bluid upsucking quhairwith blubbrit beine
His visage quhilk appeird so bauld befoir.
Far mycht he now defigurat be seine
From that renownit wordie chiftane keine,
Umquhyle the beild and piller firm of France.   600
In this estate perbrouilyit all uncleine
Upon the bounds of Spaine he cam be chance,
Quhair Angelique and Medor did avance
Thair journay rycht alongs the rivage fair;

deedlie dout fear of death
dissoverit broken up   *tours* towers   *fole* fool   *buls* bulls
beufils oxen   *raifs* raves   *rugs* tears   *glaiks* looks foolishly
bruit noise   *hurlland* hurtling   *glar* mud   *boudin* swollen
abeed remained   *boir* boar   *gobbats* pieces   *blubbrit* besmeared
bauld bold   *wordie* worthy   *keine* brave   *beild* refuge

Bot quhan the fole beheld hir beutie glance 605
Hir to persew he did with speid prepair.
Not that he knew hir persone maist preclair
Bot as ane chyld sum bonie bird wold crave
To sport thairwith and kill it syn but mair,
For sic effect fast efter hir he drave 610
And Medor all astonist did he lave,
Quhois horse lay fellit with his fist so snell.
Bot be the ring quhilk did sic vertew have
The ladie fred was from his furie fell.
This was the fole of quhom I erst did tell, 615
That rageit on the luifers passand by,
With the quhilk two no moir I will me mell.
Sum spreits poetique moir perfyt than I
To paint expertlie may thair pen apply
Quhow thay did both from thence directlie dres 620
Quhair hir great kingdome welthelie did ly,
That Medor mycht the croune thairof posses.
I lave also for to declair expres
His faictes all that did sic furie drie,
For imperfyt and tedius I confes 625
The mateir els all manckit is be me.
Waeik crezit barge upon the swelling sie
To everie wind will not hir saell upbend,
So may I not expone in ilk degrie
The histoir weill as it at lenth is pend. 630

Of Ane Symmer Hous

1   Thou bonie bour, obumbrat all with bews,
Quhairin my maistres umquhyll did delyt,
Quhan flouris fair of monie heavenlie hews
Decorit all thy plesand pairts perfyt,
Thou may lament and I with duill indyt
For laik of hir quham now, alace, we lois,
For I rejosit in hir color quhyt
And be the same thou semet moir formois.

---

preclair illustrious   *me mell* concern myself
manckit omitted   *waeik* weak
obumbrat shaded   *bews* branches   *umquhyll* once   *indyt* compose
formois beautiful

2   Quhat Nymphe or Dian sall posses the now,
         O plesand place so desolat alon?
         Thy leifs dois fead and all thy branchis bow
         For verray havie sorrow I suppon
         Because thy ladie far is from the gon,
         My solas cheiflie and thy gloir also;
         As ring quhilk lossit hes the pretious ston,
         So thou dois stand and I am vext with wo.

3   The lyvelie luisteur of hir vult devyn
         The quhilk I lang maist ernistlie to sie
         Wold schortlie eis this havie hart of myn
         That for hir absence dois sic dolor drie
         And thou, o bour, maist blissit wold thou bie
         Gif thou hir presens mycht injoy againe.
         God grant me grace that happie hour to sie
         Quhan I in the with hir may blyth remaine.

4   Thy branchis bair that now so widdrit beine
         Sall then revert fresche, flurissit and fair;
         And all thy feadit leifis grow sall greine,
         Quhair chirming birdis myrthfull sall repair;
         Than temperat salbie the celest air
         For favor of this lustie ladie brycht;
         Syn I hir awn salbie denud of cair
         In spying of so sweit ane semlie sycht.

vult face   *drie* endure   *chirming* chirping

Alexander Hume

Of the Day Estivall

1   O perfite light, quhilk schaid away
      The darkenes from the light,
      And set a ruler ou'r the day,
      Ane uther ou'r the night;

2   Thy glorie when the day foorth flies,
      Mair vively dois appeare,
      Nor at midday unto our eyes,
      The shining sun is cleare.

3   The shaddow of the earth anon,
      Remooves and drawes by,
      Sine in the East, when it is gon,
      Appeares a clearer sky.

4   Quhilk sunne perceaves the little larks,
      The lapwing and the snyp,
      And tunes their sangs like natures clarks,
      Ou'r midow, mure and stryp.

5   Bot everie bais'd nocturnall beast,
      Na langer may abide,
      They hy away baith maist and least,
      Them selves in house to hide.

6   They dread the day fra thay it see,
      And from the sight of men,
      To saits and covars fast they flee,
      As lyons to their den.

7   Oure hemisphere is poleist clein,
      And lightened more and more,
      While everie thing be clearely sein,
      Quhilk seemed dim before.

Day Estivall Summer's Day
schaid away separated   *sine* then   *snyp* snipe   *stryp* rill
bais'd dismayed   *saits and covars* homes and hiding-places

8 Except the glistering astres bright,
   Which all the night were cleere,
   Offusked with a greater light,
   Na langer dois appeare.

9 The golden globe incontinent,
   Sets up his shining head,
   And ou'r the earth and firmament,
   Displayes his beims abroad.

10 For joy the birds with boulden throts,
   Agains his visage shein,
   Takes up their kindelie musicke nots,
   In woods and gardens grein.

11 Up braids the carefull husbandman,
   His cornes and vines to see,
   And everie tymous artisan,
   In buith worke busilie.

12 The pastor quits the slouthfull sleepe,
   And passis forth with speede,
   His little camow-nosed sheepe,
   And rowtting kie to feede.

13 The passenger from perrels sure,
   Gangs gladly foorth the way:
   Briefe, everie living creature,
   Takes comfort of the day.

14 The subtile mottie rayons light,
   At rifts thay are in wonne,
   The glansing phains and vitre bright,
   Resplends against the sunne.

15 The dew upon the tender crops,
   Lyke pearles white and round,
   Or like to melted silver drops,
   Refreshes all the ground.

astres stars *offusked* obscured *incontinent* at once *boulden* swollen
braids springs *tymous* early *buith* covered stall
camow-nosed flat-nosed *rowtting* lowing *mottie* containing motes
rifts cracks *in wonne* got in *phains* vanes *vitre* window pane

16 The mystie rocke, the clouds of raine,
  From tops of mountaines skails,
  Cleare are the highest hils and plaine,
  The vapors takes the vails.

17 Begaried is the saphire pend,
  With spraings of skarlet hew,
  And preciously from end till end,
  Damasked white and blew.

18 The ample heaven of fabrik sure,
  In cleannes dois surpas,
  The chrystall and the silver pure,
  Or clearest poleist glas.

19 The time sa tranquill is and still,
  That na where sall ye find,
  Saif on ane high and barren hill,
  Ane aire of peeping wind.

20 All trees and simples great and small,
  That balmie leife do beir,
  Nor thay were painted on a wall,
  Na mair they move or steir.

21 Calme is the deepe and purpour se,
  Yee smuther nor the sand,
  The wals that woltring wont to be,
  Are stable like the land.

22 Sa silent is the cessile air,
  That every cry and call,
  The hils, and dails, and forrest fair,
  Againe repeates them all.

23 The rivers fresh, the callor streames,
  Ou'r rockes can softlie rin,
  The water cleare like chrystall seames,
  And makes a pleasant din.

---

skails clears *begaried* ornamented *pend* vault *spraings* streaks
saif except *simples* medicinal herbs *purpour* purple
smuther smoother *wals* waves *woltring* rolling *cessile* yielding
callor cool

24   The fields and earthly superfice,
With verdure greene is spread,
And naturallie but artifice,
In partie coulors cled.

25   The flurishes and fragrant flowres,
Throw Phoebus fostring heit,
Refresht with dew and silver showres,
Casts up ane odor sweit.

26   The clogged busie humming beis,
That never thinks to drowne,
On flowers and flourishes of treis,
Collects their liquor browne.

27   The sunne maist like a speedie post,
With ardent course ascends,
The beautie of the heavenly host,
Up to our zenith tends.

28   Nocht guided be na Phaeton,
Nor trained in a chyre,
Bot be the high and haly On,
Quhilk dois all where impire.

29   The burning beims downe from his face,
Sa fervently can beat:
That man and beast now seekes a place
To save them fra the heat.

30   The brethles flocks drawes to the shade,
And frechure of their fald,
The startling nolt as they were made,
Runnes to the rivers cald.

31   The heards beneath some leaffie trie,
Amids the flowers they lie,
The stabill ships upon the sey,
Tends up their sails to drie.

---

superfice surface   *partie* motley   *flurishes* blossoms
clogged burdened   *chyre* chariot   *nolt* cattle   *made* mad
tends stretches

32   The hart, the hynd and fallow deare,
          Are tapisht at their rest,
          The foules and birdes that made the beare,
          Prepares their prettie nest.

33   The rayons dures descending downe,
          All kindlis in a gleid,
          In cittie nor in borroughstowne,
          May nane set foorth their heid.

34   Back from the blew paymented whun,
          And from ilk plaister wall:
          The hote reflexing of the sun,
          Inflams the aire and all.

35   The labourers that timellie raise
          All wearie faint and weake:
          For heate downe to their houses gaise,
          Noone-meate and sleepe to take.

36   The callour wine in cave is sought,
          Mens brothing breists to cule:
          The water cald and cleare is brought,
          And sallets steipt in ule.

37   Sume plucks the honie plowm and peare,
          The cherrie and the pesche,
          Sume likes the reamand London beare,
          The bodie to refresh.

38   Forth of their skepps some raging bees,
          Lyes out and will not cast,
          Some uther swarmes hyves on the trees,
          In knots togidder fast.

39   The corbeis and the kekling kais,
          May scarce the heate abide,
          Halks prunyeis on the sunnie brais,
          And wedders back, and side.

tapisht crouching   *beare* noise   *gleid* flame
borroughstowne town   *paymented whun* whinstone made into pavement
callour fresh   *brothing* sweating   *sallets* salads   *ule* oil
reamand foaming   *skepps* hives   *corbeis* crows
kekling kais chattering jackdaws   *halks prunyeis* hawks preen

40   With gilted eyes and open wings,
             The cock his courage shawes,
             With claps of joy his breast he dings,
             And twentie times he crawes.

41   The dow with whisling wings sa blew,
             The winds can fast collect,
             Hir pourpour pennes turnes mony hew,
             Against the sunne direct.

42   Now noone is went, gaine is mid-day,
             The heat dois slake at last,
             The sunne descends downe west away,
             Fra three of clock be past.

43   A little cule of braithing wind,
             Now softly can arise,
             The warks throw heate that lay behind,
             Now men may enterprise.

44   Furth fairis the flocks to seeke their fude,
             On everie hill and plaine,
             Ilk labourer as he thinks gude,
             Steppes to his turne againe.

45   The rayons of the sunne we see,
             Diminish in their strength,
             The schad of everie towre and tree,
             Extended is in length.

46   Great is the calme for everie quhair,
             The wind is sitten downe,
             The reik thrawes right up in the air,
             From everie towre and towne.

47   Their firdoning the bony birds,
             In banks they do begin,
             With pipes of reides the jolie hirds,
             Halds up the mirrie din.

dow pigeon   *schad* shadow   *reik* smoke   *firdoning* piping

48 The maveis and the philomeen,
  The stirling whissilles loud,
  The cuschetts on the branches green,
  Full quietly they crowd.

49 The gloming comes, the day is spent,
  The sun goes out of sight,
  And painted is the occident,
  With pourpour sanguine bright.

50 The skarlet nor the golden threid,
  Who would their beautie trie,
  Are nathing like the colour reid,
  And beutie of the sky.

51 Our west horizon circuler,
  Fra time the sunne be set,
  Is all with rubies (as it wer)
  Or rosis reid ou'rfret.

52 What pleasour were to walke and see,
  Endlang a river cleare,
  The perfite forme of everie tree,
  Within the deepe appeare?

53 The salmon out of cruifs and creils
  Up hailed into skowts,
  The bels and circles on the weills,
  Throw lowpping of the trouts.

54 O! then it were a seemely thing,
  While all is still and calme,
  The praise of God to play and sing,
  With cornet and with shalme.

maveis song-thrush
philomeen nightingale *stirling* starling *cuschetts* wood-pigeons
crowd coo *gloming* twilight *ou'rfret* embroidered
cruifs fishing cruives *skowts* cobles (flat-bottomed boats) *weills* wells
shalme shawm: mediaeval instrument of oboe class

55   Bot now the hirds with mony schout,
      Cals uther be their name,
      Ga, Billie, turne our gude about,
      Now time is to go hame.

56   With bellie fow the beastes belive,
      Are turned fra the corne,
      Quhilk soberly they hameward drive,
      With pipe and lilting horne.

57   Throw all the land great is the gild,
      Of rustik folks that crie,
      Of bleiting sheepe fra they be fild,
      Of calves and routing ky.

58   All labourers drawes hame at even,
      And can till uther say,
      Thankes to the gracious God of heaven,
      Quhilk send this summer day.

gude livestock   *fow* full   *gild* clamour

Sir Robert Ayton

To His Coy Mistres

What uthers doth discourage and dismay
Is unto me a pastime and a play.
I sport in hir deneyalls and doe know
Wemen love best that doe love least in show.
Too sudden favors may abate delight   5
When modest coynes sharpes the appetite;
I grow the hotter for hir cold neglect
And more inflam'd when sho showes least respect.
Heat may aryse from rocks, from flints so fyre,
So from hir coldness I doe strik desyre.   10
Sho, knoweinge this, perhapes resolves to try
My faith and patience, offeringe to denay
What e're I aske of hir that I might be
More taken with hir for hir slightinge me.
When fishes play with baites, best, anglers say,   15
To make them bite, is drawe the baite away;
So dallies sho with me till, to my smart,
Both bait and hooke stickes fastened in my hart.
And now I am become hir foolishe prey
And that sho knowes I cannot break away,   20
Let hir resolve no longer to be free
From Cupides bondes and bind hir self to me;
Nor let hir wex me longer with dispair
That they be crewell that be younge and fair.
It is the old, the creased and the blake   25
That are unkynd and for affectione lacke.
I'le ty hir eyes with lynes, hir eares with moanes,
Hir marble hart I'le pearce with hydious groanes
That nather eyes, eares, hart sall be at rest
Till sho forsaike hir sier to love me best;   30
Nor will I raise my seige nor leave my feild
Till I have mead my valiant mistres yeeld.

The Shiphird Thirsis longed to die

The shiphird Thirsis longed to die
Gazeinge upon the gratious eye
Of hir whome he adored and loved,
When sho, whom no les passion moved,
This said, "O die not yet I pray   5
I'le die with the if thou wilt stay."
Then Thirsis for a while delayes
Tho haist he had to end his dayes,
But while he thus protractes his breathe
Not deyinge unto him was deathe.   10
At last, while languishinge he lyes
And suckes sweet nectar from hir eyes,
The lovelie shipherdes who fand
The harvest of hir love at hand
With trimblinge eyes straight falls a cryinge,   15
"Die, die sweet hart for I am dieinge."
And as the swaine did straight reply,
"Behold sweet hart with the I die,"
Thus spent these happie two there breath
In such a sweet and deathles death,   20
That they returned to lyf againe
Againe to try deathes pleasant paine.

Lov's like a Game at Irish

Lov's like a game at Irish where the dye
Of maids affection doth by fortune fly,
Which, when you thinke you certaine of the same
Proves but att best a doubtfull aftergame,
For if they finde yoar fancy in a blott   5
It's two to one if then they take you nott.
But, being gamesters, you must boldly venter
And wher you see the pointe ly open, enter.
Beleive mee one thing, nothing brings about
A game halfe lost soe soone as holding out.   10
And next to holding out, this you shall finde,
There's nothing worse then entering still behinde.

aftergame second game   *in a blott* exposed

Yet doth not all in happy entrance lye,
When you are on, you must throw home and hye.
If you throw low and weake, beleive mee then,   15
Doe what you can, they will be bearing men,
And if you looke not all the better on,
They will play false, beare two instead of one.

An Epigram

Philo lov'd Sophia and she againe
Did pay him home with coy disdaine.
Yet when he dye'd, he left her all he had.
What doe you thinke? The man was mad.

Shall Feare to seeme Untrue

Shall feare to seeme untrue
To vowes of constant duty
Make mee disgest disdaines undue
From an inconstant beautie?
Noe, I doe not affect   5
In vowes to seeme soe holy
That I would have the world to check
My constancy with folly.
Let her call breach of vow
What I call just repentance,   10
I count him base and braine sick too
That dotes on coy acquaintance.
Thus if out of her snaire
At last I doe unfold mee,
Accuse her selfe that caught me there   15
And knew not how to hold mee.
And if I rebell prove
Against my will I doe it,
Yet can I heate as well as love
When reason binds mee to it.   20

William Drummond

A Dedale of my Death

A Dedale of my death,
Now I resemble that subtile worme on earth
Which prone to its owne evill can take no rest.
For with strange thoughts possest,
I feede on fading leaves   5
Of Hope, which me deceaves,
And thousand webs doth warpe within my brest.
And thus in end unto my selfe I weave
A fast-shut prison, no, but even a grave.

Like the Idalian Queene

Like the Idalian queene
Her haire about her eyne,
With necke and brests ripe apples to be seene,
At first glance of the morne
In Cyprus gardens gathering those faire flowrs   5
Which of her bloud were borne,
I saw, but fainting saw, my paramours.
The Graces naked danc'd about the place,
The winds and trees amaz'd
With silence on her gaz'd,   10
The flowrs did smile, like those upon her face,
And as their aspine stalkes those fingers band,
(That shee might read my case)
A hyacinth I wisht mee in her hand.

A Lovers Prayer

Neare to a christall spring,
With thirst and heat opprest,
Narcissa fair doth rest;
Trees, pleasant trees which those green plaines forth bring
Now interlace your trembling tops above   5
And make a canopie unto my love,
So in heavens highest house when sunne appeares,
Aurora may you cherish with her teares.

The Qualitie of a Kisse

The kisse with so much strife,
Which I late got (sweet heart)
Was it a signe of Death, or was it Life?
Of Life it could not bee,
For I by it did sigh my soule in thee,   5
Nor was it Death, Death doth no joy impart:
Thou silent stand'st, ah! what thou didst bequeath,
To mee a dying Life was, living Death.

Upon a Glasse

If thou wouldst see threedes purer than the gold,
Where Love his wealth doth show,
But take this glasse, and thy faire haire behold:
If whitenesse thou wouldst see more white than snow,
And reade on Wonders booke,   5
Take but this glasse, and on thy forehead looke:
Wouldst thou in Winter see a crimsin rose,
Whose thornes doe hurt each heart,
Looke but in glasse how thy sweet lips doe close:
Wouldst thou see planets which all good impart,   10
Or meteores divine?
But take this glasse, and gaze upon thine eine:
No, planets, rose, snow, gold, cannot compare
With you, deare eyes, lips, browes, and amber haire.

It was the Time when to our Northerne Pole

It was the time when to our Northerne Pole
The brightest lampe of heaven beginnes to rolle,
When Earth more wanton in new robes appeareth,
And scorning skies her flowrs in rain-bowes beareth,
On which the aire moist saphires doth bequeath,   5
Which quake to feele the kissing Zephires breath:
When birds from shadie groves their love foorth warble,
And sea like heaven, heaven lookes like smoothest marble,
When I, in simple course, free from all cares,
Farre from the muddie worlds captiving snares,   10

By Oras flowrie bancks alone did wander,
Ora that sports her like to old Meander,
A floud more worthie fame and lasting praise
Than that which Phaetons fall so high did raise:
Into whose mooving glasse the milk-white lillies   15
Doe dresse their tresses and the daffadillies.
Where Ora with a wood is crown'd about
And seemes forget the way how to come out,
A place there is, where a delicious fountaine
Springs from the swelling paps of a proud mountaine,   20
Whose falling streames the quiet caves doe wound,
And make the ecchoes shrill resound that sound.
The laurell there the shining channell graces,
The palme her love with long-stretch'd armes embraces,
The poplar spreds her branches to the skie,   25
And hides from sight that azure cannopie.
The streames the trees, the trees their leaves still nourish,
That place grave winter finds not without flourish.
If living eyes Elysian fields could see
This little Arden might Elysium bee.   30
Here Diane often used to repose her,
And Acidalias queene with Mars rejoyce her:
The nymphes oft here doe bring their maunds with flowres,
And anadeames weave for their paramours,
The satyres in those shades are heard to languish,   35
And make the shepheards partners of their anguish,
The shepheards who in barkes of tender trees
Doe grave their loves, disdaines and jelousies,
Which Phillis when there by her flockes she feedeth
With pitie whyles, sometime with laughter reedeth.   40
    Neare to this place when sunne in midst of day,
In highest top of heaven his coach did stay,
And (as advising) on his carier glanced
The way did rest, the space he had advanced
His panting steeds along those fields of light,   45
Most princely looking from that gastly hight:
When most the grashoppers are heard in meadowes,
And loftie pines have small, or els no shadowes,
It was my hap, O wofull hap! to bide
Where thickest shades me from all rayes did hide   50
Into a shut-up-place, some Sylvans chamber,

maunds wicker baskets   *anadeames* garlands

Whose seeling spred was with the lockes of amber
Of new-bloom'd sicamors, floore wrought with flowres,
More sweete and rich than those in princes bowres.
Here Adon blush't and Clitia all amazed   55
Lookt pale, with him who in the fountaine gazed,
The Amaranthus smyl'd and that sweet boy
Which sometime was the God of Delos joy,
The brave carnation, speckled pinke here shined,
The violet her fainting head declined,   60
Beneath a drowsie chasbow, all of gold
The marigold her leaves did here unfold.
    Now while that ravish'd with delight and wonder,
Halfe in a trance I lay those arches under,
The season, silence, place did all entise   65
Eyes heavie lids to bring night on their skies,
Which softly having stollen themselves together
(Like evening clouds) me plac'd I wote not whether.
As cowards leave the fort which they should keepe
My senses one by one gave place to sleepe,   70
Who followed with a troupe of golden slombers
Thrust from my quiet braine all base encombers,
And thrise me touching with his rod of gold,
A heaven of visions in my temples roll'd
To countervaile those pleasures were bereft me,   75
Thus in his silent prison clos'd he left me.
. . .

The Country Maid

A country maid amazon-like did ryde,
To sit more sure with legge on either syde;
Her mother who her spyed, sayd that ere long
Shee might due pennance suffer for that wrong,
For when tyme should more yeeres on her bestow   5
That horses hair between her thighes would grow.
Scarce winter twice was come as was her told,
When shee found all to frizell there with gold,
Which first her made affraid then turnd her sicke
And keept her in her bed almost a weeke.   10

chasbow poppy   *encombers* burdens

At last her mother calls, who scarce for laughter
Could heare the pleasant storie of her daughter;
But that this thought no longer should her vex
She said that barded thus was all the sex;
And to prove true that now shee did not scorne,   15
Reveald to her the gate where shee was borne.
The girle, that seeing, cryed, now freed of paine,
"Ah, mother, yee have ridden on the maine!"

A Jest

In a most holy church, a holy man,
Unto a holy Saint, with visage wan,
And eyes like fountaines, mumbled forth a prayer,
And with strange words, and sighes, made blacke the aire:
And having long so stay'd, and long long pray'd,   5
A thousand crosses on himselfe hee lay'd,
Then with some sacred beads hung on his arme,
His eyes, his mouth, brest, temples did hee charme.
Thus not content (strange worship hath none end)
To kisse the earth at last hee did pretend,   10
And bowing downe, besought with humble grace
An aged woman neere to give some place:
She turn'd, and turning up her pole beneath,
Said, "Sir, kisse heere, for it is all but earth."

Great God, *whom Wee with Humble Thoughts adore*

Great God, whom wee with humble thoughts adore,
Eternall, infinite, almightie King,
Whose dwellings Heaven transcend, whose throne before
Archangells serve, and Seraphines doe sing;
Of nought who wrought all that with wondring eyes   5
Wee doe behold within this spacious round,
Who makes the rockes to rocke, to stand the skies,
At whose command clouds dreadfull thunders sound:
Ah! spare us wormes, weigh not how wee (alas!)
(Evill to our selves) against thy lawes rebell,   10
Wash of those spots, which still in mindes cleare glasse
(Though wee bee loath to looke) wee see to well.

barded bearded

Deserv'd revenge, o doe not, doe not take,
Doe thou revenge what shall abide thy blow?
Passe shall this world, this world which thou didst make,   15
Which should not perish till thy trumpet blow.
What soule is found whom parents crime not staines?
Or what with its owne sinne destaind is not?
Though Justice rigor threaten (ah) her raines
Let Mercy guide, and never bee forgot.   20
   Lesse are our faults farre farre than is thy love,
O! what can better seeme thy grace divine,
Than they that plagues deserve thy bounty prove,
And where thou showre makst vengeance faire to shine?
Then looke and pittie, pittying forgive   25
Us guiltie slaves, or servants, now in thrall,
Slaves, if (alas) thou looke how wee doe live;
Or doing ill or doing nought at all?
Of an ungratefull minde a foule effect!
But if thy giftes which amplie heretofore   30
Thou hast upon us powr'd thou dost respect,
Wee are thy servants, nay, than servants more;
Thy children, yes, and children dearely bought.
But what strange chance us of this lot bereaves?
Poore worthles wights how lowlie are wee brought,   35
Whom grace made children, sinne hath turned slaves:
Sinne hath turn'd slaves, but let those bands grace breake,
That in our wrongs thy mercies may appeare,
Thy wisedome not so meane is, pow'r so weake,
But thousand wayes they can make worlds thee feare.   40
   O wisedome boundlesse! O miraculous grace!
Grace, wisedome which make winke dimme reasons eye,
And could Heavens King bring from his placelesse place,
On this ignoble stage of care to die:
To dye our death, and with the sacred streame   45
Of bloud and water guishing from his side,
To put away each odious act and blame,
By us contriv'd, or our first parents pride.
Thus thy great love and pitty (heavenly King)
Love, pitty, which so well our losse prevent,   50
Of evill it selfe (loe!) could all goodnesse bring,
And sad beginning cheare with glad event.
O Love and pitty! ill-knowne of these times,
O Love and pittie! carefull of our neede,
O bounties! which our execrable crimes   55

(Now numberlesse) contend neere to exceed.
Make this excessive ardour of thy love,
So warme our coldnesse, so our lifes renew,
That wee from sinne, sinne may from us remove,
Wit may our will, faith may our wit subdue.   60
Let thy pure Love burne up all wordly lust,
Hells pleasant poison killing our best part,
Which makes us joye in toyes, adore fraile dust
In stead of Thee, in temple of our heart.
　　Grant when at last our soules these bodies leave,   65
Their loathsome shops of sinne and mansions blinde,
And Doome before thy royall seat receave,
They may a Saviour, not a judge thee finde.

Doome Judgment

Sir William Mure

The Cry of Blood and of a Broken Covenant

What horrid actings force unwilling ears
With worst of news? Do fancies and fond fears
Mock troubled minds or doth a reall blow
For preface passe to Albion's overthrow?
Have parricids, professing brother-hood,   5
Put hand in Caesar, shed his royall bloud,
Low in the dust this Islands glory laid
And, at one stroak, her children orphans made?
   O Heavens! O Earth! heer I must pause a space.
Griefs tide flows higher, then, in this sad case,   10
Can calm'd be by expression. But, to speak
Allegiance pleads. Men soberest, minds most meek,
Most free of passion, cannot but resent
This high Injustice; yea, in freedome vent
Their thoughts and what a dialect to use,   15
This bloody prelude speaks. Then free-born Muse
Tell Britaine, tell the World, that hence, in vain
Words shall be heard of any milder straine
Then martiall eloquence. In trumpets sound
Be Scotlands musick henceforth deeply drown'd!   20
From Heav'ns th'alarme, attended orders bee,
All doubts discust, all judgments clear and free!
   Let colours fly, drums beat. Gird on your swords.
   Arme gallants, arme! The battell is the Lords!
. . .

Robert Sempill

The Life and Death of Habbie Simson the Piper of Kilbarchan

1   Kilbarchan now may say, alas!
    For she hath lost her game and grace,
    Both "Trixie" and "The Maiden Trace";
    But what remead?
    For no man can supply his place,
    Hab Simson's dead.

2   Now who shall play "The Day it Daws"?
    Or "Hunts Up", when the cock he craws?
    Or who can for our Kirk-town-cause,
    Stand us in stead?
    On bagpipes (now) no body blaws,
    Sen Habbie's dead.

3   Or wha will cause our shearers shear?
    Wha will bend up "The Brags of Weir",
    Bring in the bells or good play meir,
    In time of need?
    Hab Simson cou'd, what needs you speer?
    But (now) he's dead.

4   So kindly to his neighbours neast,
    At Beltan and Saint Barchan's feast
    He blew, and then held up his breast,
    As he were weid;
    But now we need not him arrest,
    For Habbie's dead.

5   At fairs he play'd before the spear-men,
    All gaily graithed in their gear men.
    Steell bonnets, jacks and swords so clear then
    Like any bead.
    Now wha shall play before such weir-men,
    Sen Habbie's dead?

---

remead cure	*bend up* begin to play	*speer* ask	*weid* mad
graithed arrayed	*weir-men* men of war		

6   At Clark plays when he wont to come,
His pipe play'd trimly to the drum;
Like bikes of bees he gart it bum
And tun'd his reed.
Now all our pipers may sing dumb,
Sen Habbie's dead.

7   And at horse races many a day,
Before the black, the brown, the gray,
He gart his pipe, when he did play,
Baith skirl and skreed:
Now all such pastimes quite away,
Sen Habbie's dead.

8   He counted was a wail'd wight-man,
And fiercely at foot-ball he ran:
At every game the gree he wan,
For pith and speed.
The like of Habbie was na than,
But now he's dead.

9   And than, besides his valiant acts,
At bridals he wan many placks,
He bobbed ay behind fo'ks backs
And shook his head.
Now we want many merry cracks,
Sen Habbie's dead.

10   He was convoyer of the bride
With Kittock hinging at his side:
About the kirk he thought a pride
The ring to lead.
But now we may gae but a guide
For Habbie's dead.

bikes hives   *bum* hum
skirl shrill   *skreed* screech   *wail'd wight-man* chosen stalwart
gree victory   *placks* farthings   *cracks* capers   *gae but* go without

11   So well's he keeped his 'decorum',
        And all the stots of "Whip-meg-morum";
        He slew a man, and wae's me for him,
        And bure the fead!
        But yet the man wan hame before him,
        And was not dead!

12   Ay whan he play'd, the lasses leugh,
        To see him teethless, auld and teugh.
        He wan his pipes beside Borcheugh,
        Withoutten dread:
        Which after wan him gear enough;
        But now he's dead.

13   Ay whan he play'd, the gaitlings gedder'd,
        And when he spake the carl bledder'd;
        On Sabbath days his cap was fedder'd,
        A seemly weid.
        In the kirk-yeard his mare stood tedder'd,
        Where he lies dead.

14   Alas! for him my heart is sair,
        For of his springs I gat a skair,
        At every play, race, feast and fair,
        But guile or greed.
        We need not look for pyping mair,
        Sen Habbie's dead.

---

stots beats (of a tune)   *bure* bore   *fead* feud   *leugh* laughed
teugh tough   *gaitlings gedder'd* children gathered
carl bledder'd old man blethered   *fedder'd* feathered   *weid* garment
springs lively tunes   *skair* share

THE SONNET

James VI

1   That blessed houre, when first was broght to light
Our earthlie Juno and our gratious Queene,
Three goddesses how soone they hade her seene
Contended who protect her shoulde by right,
Bot being as goddesses of equall might
And as of female sexe like stiffe in will,
It was agreed by sacred Phoebus skill
To joyne there powers to blesse that blessed wight.
Then happie monarch, sprung of Ferguse race,
That talkes with wise Minerve when pleaseth the
And when thou list sum princelie sporte to see,
Thy chaste Diana rides with the in chase,
Then, when to bed thou gladlie does repaire,
Clasps in thine armes thy Cytherea faire.

2   Although that crooked, crawling Vulcan lie
An-under ashes colde as oft we see,
As senseles deade, whill by his heate he drie
The greene and fizzing faggots made of tree,
Then will that litle sponke and flaming eye
Bleaze bravelie forth and, sparkling all abreed
With wandling up a wondrous sight to see,
Kithe clearlie then and on the faggots feede.
So am I forced for to confesse indeede,
My sponke of love, smor'd under coales of shame,
By beauties force, the fosterer of that seede,
Now budds and bursts in an appearing flame;
Bot since your beautie hath this wonder wroght,
I houpe Madame it shall not be for noght.

wight person   *sponke* spark   *abreed* abroad   *wandling* flickering
smor'd smothered

3 Haill mirthfull May the moneth full of joye!
   Haill mother milde of hartsume herbes and flowres!
   Haill fostrer faire of everie sporte and toye
   And of Auroras dewis and summer showres!
   Haill friend to Phoebus and his glancing houres!
   Haill sister scheine to Nature breeding all,
   Who by the raine that cloudie skies out pouris
   And Titans heate, reformes the faided fall
   In woefull winter by the frostie gall
   Of sadd Saturnus tirrar of the trees!
   And now by Natures might and thine, they shall
   Be florish'd faire with colours that agrees;
   Then lett us all be gladd to honour the,
   As in olde tymes was ever wonte to be.

4 All kinde of wronge allace it now aboundes
   And honestie is fleemed out of this land;
   Now trumprie ouer trueth his triumphe soundes;
   Who now can knowe the hart by tongue or hand?
   Cummes ever justice at the barre to stande?
   Where can she be in these our later dayes?
   Alike in water for to wagg a wande
   As speare for her if truelie sundrie sayes,
   For manie now abroade doe daylie blaize
   That justice hath her hart infected sore.
   How can she then be cleane in anie wayes
   Bot must become corrupted more and more?
   Sume lockman now hath locked up apart
   Poore justice, martyr'd with a meschant hart.

John Stewart of Baldynneis

5 Fresche fontane fair and springand cald and cleine
   As brychtest christall cleir with silver ground,
   Close cled about be holsum herbis greine,
   Quhois twynkling streames yeilds ane luiflie sound;
   With bonie birkis all ubumbrat round
   From violence of Phebus visage fair,

scheine bright *tirrar* stripper *fleemed* banished
wagg wave *wande* stick *speare* ask *meschant* miserable
ubumbrat shaded

Quhois smelling leifs suave Zephir maks rebound
In doucest souching of his temperat air;
And Titan new hich flammyng in his chair
Maks gaggit erth for ardent heit to brist.
Than passinger, quho irkit dois repair,
Brynt be the son and dryit up with thrist,
Heir in this place thou may refreschment find
Both be the well, the schaddow and the wind.

6   As dryest dust – winddrift in drouthie day –
Quhyls lychts on lords and ladies of renoune,
Quhyls on thair face and quhyls on thair array
And quhyls upon ane kingis statlie croune;
Yit as it cums sum ay are bussie boune
To cleinge it thence, so that it finds no rest
Quhill to the erth it be againe snipt doune:
So mortall men, quho dois thair mynd molest
To be in gloir coequall with the best,
Thocht for ane space thay volt with waltring wind,
Doune to the ground thay sall againe be drest,
For few aloft may fortouns firmtie find.
Bot ay the swyfter and moir hich thay brall,
Moir low and suddane cums thair feirfull fall.

7   Guid day madam, with humyll thanks also,
That me unto your ludgeing lairge did gyd.
Yea, skairs I knew quhan I thairin did go
Quhair I sould wend, the wallis war so wyd.
Thocht than I slippit, quhan ye bad me byd,
Excuise my part, the falt was not in me;
Your pathed pathment meid my paessis slyd,
That I was forst to bow upon my kne.
Bot yit I thank you of your ludgeing frie,
I grant in deid ye hold ane oppine port,
Bot inexpert I am to swym the sie,
Quhilk flows on bordor of your brod resort,
Quhairin I wat is furnissing but dout
To serve the Turck and all his camp about!

---

souching moaning   *chair* chariot   *gaggit* cracked
brist burst   *winddrift* wind driven   *bussie boune* busily ready
volt rise up   *waltring* tossing   *brall* soar   *humyll* humble
pathment pavement

8   Luif is ane aigre, douce delyt and greif:
Greif is in luif ane lustie langing lyf:
Lyf may not last quhair luif pretends mischeif:
Mischeif of luif is evirlasting stryf:
Stryf reuling luif than rancor raidgeis ryf:
Ryf raidge is not, gif luifers luif abound:
Abounding luif is scharp as scharpest knyf:
Knyf may not kill moir scharplie with ane wound:
Wound deip with wo and schortlie haill and sound,
Sound syn to swell in syching sour and sweit,
Sweit luif heirwith dois suffer monie stound,
Stound both with cair and confort lairge repleit:
Repleit with luif hes bein both gods and men:
Men luif obeyis, gods will not luif misken.

9   O silver hornit Diane nychtis queine,
Quha for to kis Endimeon did discend,
Gif flamme of luif thou haid don than susteine,
As I do now, that instant dois pretend
T'embrasse my luif not willing to be kend,
With mistie vaill thou wold obscuir thy face
For reuth of me that dois sic travell spend,
And finding now this vissit grant of grace,
Bot lettit be thy borrowit lycht alace,
I staying stand in feir for to be seine,
Sen yndling eine invirons all this place,
Quhois cursit mouths ay to defame dois meine.
Bot nether thay nor yit thy schyning cleir
May cause appeir my secreit luif synceir.

10   Dull dolor dalie dois delyt destroy,
Will wantith wit waist worn with wickit wo,
Cair cankert causith confortles convoy,
Seveir sad sorrow scharplie schoris so,
My myrthles mynd may mervell monie mo;
Promp peirles proper plesand perll preclair,
Fair fremmit freind, firm fellest frownyng fo,

---

aigre bitter	*stound* ache	*misken* misunderstand
grant of favoured by	*lettit* hindered	*yndling* jealous
convoy companion	*promp* assist	*fremmit* distant

Ryche rubie rycht renownit royall rair,
Send succor soone so suadge sall sourest sair,
Grant grivous gronyng gratious guerdon guid,
For favor flowing from fresche faces fair
Restoris rychtlie restles rancor ruid,
Bot beutie breding bittir boudin baill
Dois dalie deedlie dwynyng dartis daill.

Alexander Montgomerie

11   Iniquitie on eirth is so increst,
All flesh bot few with falset is defyld,
Givin ou'r of God, with gredynes beguyld
So that the puir, but pitie, ar opprest.
God in his justice dou na mair digest
Sik sinfull swyn with symonie defyld
But must revenge, thair vyces ar so vyld,
And pour doun plagues of famin, sword and pest.
Aryse O Lord, delyver from the lave
Thy faithfull flock befor that it infect!
Thou sees how Satan sharps for to dissave,
If it were able, even thyn awin elect.
Sen conscience, love and cheritie all laiks,
Lord, short the season for the chosens saiks.

12   A Baxters bird, a bluiter beggar borne,
Ane ill heud huirsone lyk a barkit hyde,
A saulles swinger, sevintie tymes mensworne,
A peltrie pultron poyson'd up with pryde,
A treuthles tongue that turnes with eviry tyde,
A double deillar with dissait indeud,
A luiker bak whare he wes bund to byde,
A retrospicien whom the Lord outspeud,
A brybour baird that mekle baill hes breud,
Ane hypocrit, ane ydill atheist als,

boudin grievous   *daill* distribute
falset falsehood   *swyn* swine   *lave* rest   *sharps* plays tricks
laiks are lacking   *bluiter* babbler   *heud huirsone* baptised bastard
swinger scoundrel   *mensworne* perjured   *peltrie pultron* paltry coward
brybour baird exposed taker of bribes

A skurvie skybell for to be esheu'd,
A faithles, fekles, fingerles and fals,
A Turk that tint Tranent for the Tolbuith.
Quha reids this riddill, he is sharpe forsuith.

13   Remembers thou in Aesope of a taill?
A loving dog wes of his maister fane;
To fawn on him wes all his pastym haill.
His courteous maister clappit him agane.
By stood ane asse, a beist of blunter brane.
Perceiving this, bot looking to no freet,
To pleis hir maister with the counterpane,
Sho clambe on him with hir foull clubbit feet,
To play the messan thoght sho wes not [meit].
Sho meinit weill I grant; hir mynd wes guid,
Bot whair sho troude hir maister suld hir [treit],
They battound hir whill that they saw hir b[luid].
So stands with me, who loves with all my [hairt]
My maister best; some taks it in ill pai[rt.]

14   So swete a kis yistrene fra thee I reft
In bowing down thy body on the bed,
That evin my lyfe within thy lippis I left.
Sensyne from thee my spirits wald never shed;
To folow thee it from my body fled
And left my corps als cold as ony kie.
Bot when the danger of my death I dred,
To seik my spreit I sent my harte to thee;
Bot it wes so inamored with thyn ee,
With thee it myndit lykwyse to remane;
So thou hes keepit captive all the thrie,
More glaid to byde then to returne agane.
Except thy breath thare places had suppleit,
Even in thyn armes thair doutles had I deit.

15   Swete nichtingale, in holene grene that han[ts]
To sport thy self and speciall in the spri[ng];
Thy chivring chirlis, whilks chainginglie thou [chants],
Maks all the roches round about the ring,

---

skurvie skybell worthless fellow
tint left   *freet* omen   *counterpane* like   *messan* lap-dog
battound beat   *sensyne* afterwards   *kie* key   *holene* holly
chivring chirlis quivering trills

Whilk slaiks my sorow so to heir the sing
And lights my loving langour at the leist.
Yit thoght thou sees not, sillie, saikles thing,
The peircing pykis brods at thy bony breist.
Evin so am I by plesur lykwyis preist,
In gritest danger whair I most delyte.
Bot since thy song for shoring hes not ceist,
Suld feble I, for feir, my conqueis quyt?
Na, na – I love the freshest Phoenix fair,
In beuty, birth, in bounty but compair!

16   The lesbian lad, that weirs the wodbind wr[eath]
With Ceres and Cylenus, gled your ging.
Be blyth Kilburnie with the bairns of Be[ath]
And let Lochwinnoch lordie lead your rin[g]!
Be mirrie men, feir God and serve the Ki[ng]
And cair not by Dame Fortuns fead a fl[ea]!
Syne, welcome hame swete Semple sie ye sin[g],
Gut ou'r and let the wind shute in the s[ea]!
I Richie, Jane and George are lyk to d[ee],
Four crabit crippilis crackand in our crouch.
Sen I am trensh-man for the other thrie,
Let drunken Pancrage drink to me in D[utch].
Scol frie, al out, albeit that I suld brist
Ih wachts, hale beir, fan hairts and nych[sum] drist.

17   I dreamit ane dreame, o that my dreame wer trew!
Me thocht my maistres to my chalmer came
And with hir harmeles handis the cowrteingis drew
And sweitlie callit on me be my name.
"Art ye on sleip," quod sche, "o fy for schame!
Have ye nocht tauld that luifaris takis no rest?"
Me thocht I answerit, "Trew it is my dame,
I sleip nocht so your luif dois me molest."
With that me thocht hir nicht-gowne of sche cuist,
Liftit the claiss and lichtit in my armis;
Hir rosie lippis me thocht on me sche thrist
And said, "May this nocht stanche you of your harmes!"
"Mercy Madame," me thocht I menit to say,
Bot quhen I walkennit, alace, sche was away.

brods pricks   *shoring* threatening
gled gladdens   *ging* company   *fead* enmity   *crackand* gossiping
crouch crouching-place   *trensh-man* spokesman   *chalmer* chamber
tauld said   *cuist* cast   *claiss* bedclothes

William Fowler

18   The day is done, the sunn dothe ells declyne,
Night now approaches and the moone appeares,
The twinkling starrs in firmament dois schyne,
Decoring with the poolles there circled spheres;
The birds to nests, wyld beasts to denns reteirs,
The moving leafes unmoved now repose,
Dew dropps dois fall, the portraicts of my teares,
The waves within the seas theme calmlye close:
To all things nature ordour dois impose
Bot not to love that proudlye doith me thrall,
Quha all the dayes and night, but chainge or choyse,
Steirs up the coales of fyre unto my fall
And sawes his breirs and thornes within my hart,
The fruits quhairoff ar duble greiff, grones and smart.

19   I walk within this wood to vent my woes,
Remembring all my greiffs and endles grones,
Whils growing joyes deip sad conceates orgoes
And loades my hart with love and mynde with mones;
The playsant singing birds my plaints expones;
My teares from springs and wells semes to discend;
Yea, baith the highest hills and hardest stones,
Gif eare they have, a eare to me extend.
Then att the aeks and allers that perpend
My plaints I speire, quhat way will they me feid,
If for to stey with theme I condiscend:
"On grene," say they, "for grene dois hope ay breid,
Which fedethe wrachles as by proofe they prove
And brings disparing saules some ease in love."

20   O nights, no nights bot ay a daylye payne!
O dayes, no dayes bot cluddie nights obscure!
O lyfe most lothd, transchangd in deathe againe!
O doole, no doole but certain deathe and suire!
O harte, no harte bot rok and marble dure
Quhair waves of woe with tempests stryketh soare!

---

decoring adorning	*poolles* poles	*conceates* fancies	*orgoes* conquer
expones expound	*aeks* oaks	*allers* alders	

O eyes, which ay against my harte conteure!
O teares, no teares bot of salt streames the store!
O heavens, no heavens bot cahos of disglore!
O godds, the guyders of my best hard happ!
O dame, quho dothe depress all reuthe and smore!
O nights, day, lyfe, o doole of deathe the trapp,
O harte, o eyes, o teares, o godds and dame,
Quhen sal her frosts be warmed be my flame?

21   Even as the foolisch fliee, quhase custome is
By flams to fyre her wings and lyfe to lose,
Dothe fondlye flie to her conceated bliss
And purches deathe in place of her repose,
So in beholding thee, my fragrant rose,
Thy sweit aspect hethe quikned up desyre,
Which of my ruiyne doth the cause disclose
And forceth me for to refanne my fyre;
So that in this for quhilk we bothe aspyre,
We equall doole and disadvantage prove;
With lyke effects of our imagind hyre
We lose our lyfe and onlye bot by love.
Disequall yet in this ar thou and I;
Thou quicklyee dees, I deing never die.

22   Upon the utmost corners of the warld
And on the borders of this massive round,
Quhaire fates and fortoune hither hes me harld,
I doe deplore my greiffs upon this ground,
And seing roring seis from roks rebound
By ebbs and streames of contrair routing tyds
And Phebus chariot in there waves ly dround,
Quha equallye now night and day devyds,
I cal to mynde the storms my thoughts abyds,
Which ever wax and never dois decress,
For nights of dole dayes joys ay ever hyds
And in there vayle doith al my weill suppress:
So this I sie; quhaire ever I remove,
I chainge bot sees, but can not chainge my love.

---

disglore dishonour   *smore* extinguish   *conceated* imagined
harld dragged   *routing* roaring

Sir William Alexander

23   Huge hosts of thoughts imbattled in my brest,
Are ever busied with intestine warres,
And like to Cadmus earth-borne troupes at jarres,
Have spoil'd my soule of peace, themselves of rest.
Thus forc'd to reape such seed as I have sowne,
I (having interest in this doubtfull strife)
Hope much, feare more, doubt most, unhappie life.
What ever side prevaile, I'm still orethrowne:
O neither life nor death! ô both, but bad
Imparadiz'd, whiles in mine owne conceit,
My fancies straight againe imbroyle my state,
And in a moment make me glad and sad.
Thus neither yeelding quite to this nor that,
I live, I die, I do I wot not what.

24   O now I thinke, and do not thinke amisse,
That th'old philosophers were all but fooles,
Who us'd such curious questions in their schooles,
Yet could not apprehend the highest blisse.
Lo, I have learn'd in th'Academe of Love,
A maxime which they never understood:
To love and be belov'd, this is the good,
Which for most sov'raigne all the world will prove,
That which delights us most must be our treasure:
And to what greater joy can one aspire,
Then to possesse all that he doth desire,
Whil'st two united soules do melt in pleasure?
This is the greatest good can be invented,
That is so great it cannot be augmented.

25   Oft have I heard, which now I must deny,
That nought can last if that it be extreame;
Times dayly change, and we likewise in them,
Things out of sight do straight forgotten die:
There is nothing more vehement then love,
And yet I burne, and burne still with one flame.
Times oft have chang'd, yet I remaine the same,
Nought from my mind her image can remove:

at jarres at variance

The greatnesse of my love aspires to ruth,
Time vowes to crowne my constancie in th'end,
And absence doth my fancies but extend;
Thus I perceive the poet spake the truth,
That who to see strange countries were inclin'd,
Might change the aire, but never change the mind.

26   Awake my muse and leave to dreame of loves,
Shake off soft fancies chaines, I must be free,
Ile perch no more upon the mirtle tree,
Nor glide through th'aire with beauties sacred doves;
But with Joves stately bird Ile leave my nest,
And trie my sight against Apolloes raies:
Then if that ought my ventrous course dismaies,
Upon the olives boughes Ile light and rest:
Ile tune my accents to a trumpet now,
And seeke the laurell in another field.
Thus I that once, as beautie meanes did yeeld,
Did divers garments on my thoughts bestow,
Like Icarus I feare, unwisely bold,
Am purpos'd others passions now t'unfold.

Sir David Murray

27   My Caelia sat once by a christal brooke,
Gazing how smoothly the cleere streams did slide,
Who had no sooner her sweet sight espi'd,
When with amazement they did on her looke.
The waters slyding by her seem'd to mourne,
Desirous stil for to behold her beauty,
Neglecting to the ocean their duty,
In thousand strange meanders made returne;
But oh! againe with what an heavenly tune,
Those pleasant streames that issued from the spring,
To see that goddesse did appeare to sing,
Whom having view'd did as the first had done.
If those pure streams delighted so to eye her,
Judge how my soule doth surfet when I see her.

28   Gazing from out the windowes of mine eyes,
To view the object of my hearts desire,
My famish'd lookes in wandring troupes forth flies,
Hoping by some good fortune to espie her;
But having flowne with staring wings long space,
And missing still the aime that caus'd them soare,
Scorning to feed on any other face,
Turnes to their cabins backe and flies no more,
And there enclos'd disdaines to view the light,
Shadowing my face with sable cloudes of griefe:
And thus I breath in cares continuall night,
Till that her sight afford me some reliefe.
Sweet, then make hast these cloudy cares to cleare
And glad those eyes that holds thy sight so deare.

29   Stay passenger and with relenting looke,
Behold heere Bellizarius, I pray,
Whom never-constant fortune, changing aye,
Even at the top of greatnesse quite forsooke,
And, which is wondrous, in a moment tooke
Mee from the hight of an imperiall sway,
And plac'd me heere, blind begging by this way,
Whose greatnesse somtime scarce the world could brook.
And while thou daignes thy pittifull aspect,
Ah sorrow not so much my fortunes past,
As I beseech thee to bewaile this last!
That from such honour abjectlie deject,
I yet am forc'd a spectacle to live,
Glad to receive the meanest almes thou't give.

Alexander Craig

30   O watchfull bird proclaymer of the day,
Withhold I pray thy piercing notes from me:
Yet crow and put the pilgrime to his way
And let the worke-man rise to earn his fee:
Yea let the lion fierce be feard of thee,
To leave his prey and lodge him in his cave:
And let the deepe divine from dreaming flie,
To looke his leaves within his close conclave:

looke read

Each man, save I, may some remembrance have,
That gone is night and Phospher draweth nie:
Beat not thy breast for mee poor sleepeles slave,
To whom the fates alternall rest denie:
But if thou wouldst bring truce unto my teares,
Crow still for mercie in my mistris eares.

31   The Persian king in danger to be dround,
Ask'd if no helpe in humane hands did stand.
The skipper then cast in the salt profound
Some Persians brave and brought the king to land.
Then Xerxes crowns the skipper with his hand,
"Who saves the king deserv's," quoth he, "a crowne."
But he at once to kill him gave command,
"Die, die," said he, "who did my Persians drowne."
My ladie faire a Xerxes proud doth prove,
My worthless verse she doth reward with gold,
But, O allace, she lets me die for love
And now I rew that I have bin so bold.
As Xerxes crownd and kild his man, right so
Shee seemes a friend and proves a mortall foe.

32   How oft hast thou with siuet smelling breath,
Told how thou lovd'st me, lovd'st me best of al;
And to repay my love, my zeale, my fayth,
Said to thy captive thou wast but a thrall?
And when I would for comfort on thee call,
"Be true to mee deare to my soule," said I;
Then sweetly quhespering would thou say, "I shall,"
And echo-like, "deare to my soule," replie.
But breach of fayth now seemes no fault to thee,
Old promises new perjuries do prove.
Apes turfe the whelps they love from tree to tree
And crush them to the death with too much love.
My too much love I see hath chang'd thee so,
That from a friend thou art become a foe.

33   When Alexander did subdue and bring
The coastly iles of Inde to his empire,
Hee captive tooke proud Porus, Indian king,
And bid him aske what most he did desire.

quhespering whispering

"Nought," said brave Porus, "do I now require
But that thou use me as a king should bee."
"Thou shalt have friendly hostage to thy hyre
And for my sake I graunt thy sute," said hee.
Long with my passions have I borne debate,
Oft have I fought and now have lost the feeld,
It is my fortune for to be defeate.
I am thy captive and, faire dame, I yeeld:
As Macedon was to the King of Inde,
If not mine, yet for thy cause be kinde.

34   My wandring verse hath made thee known allwhare,
Thou known by them and they are known by mee:
Thou, they and I a true relation beare,
As but the one an other can not bee;
For if it chance by thy disdane I die,
My songs shal cease and thou be known no more.
Thus by experience thou mayst plainly see,
I them, thou mee, and they do thee decore.
Thou art that dame whom I shall ay adore
In spight of fortune and the frowning fates,
Whose shining beautie makes my songs to sore
In hyperbolik, loftie, heigh conceits:
Thou, they and I throughout the world be known;
They mine, thou theirs and last I am thine own.

Sir Robert Ayton

35   Pamphilia hath a number of gud pairtes
Which comendatione to hir worth impairtes
But amongest all, in one sho doth excell,
That sho can paint inimitablie well;
And yet so modest that if praisd for this
Sho'le sweare sho doth not know what paintinge is,
But straight will blush with such a pretie grace
That one wold think vermelion dyed hir face.
One of hir pictures I have oftymes seene
And wold have sworne that it hir self had bein,
Yet when I bade hir it one me bestowe,
I'le sweare I hard the picturs self say no.
What, think you this a prodegie? It's non;
The painter and the picture were both one.

decore invest with honour   *pairtes* accomplishments

36   I bid farewell unto the world and thee,
To the because thou art extreame unkinde,
Unto the world, because the world to me
Is nothing, since I cannott move thy minde.
Were any mercy in thy soule inshrin'd,
Could sighes or teares make soft thy flinty heart,
I could perhapps more easily be inclin'd
To spend my dayes with the then to depart.
But since thou knowes not Cupids golden dart
But hath been wounded with a shaft of lead,
It is but folly to pretend his art
To sue for favour, when I finde but feade.
Soe farewell Nimph, farewell for aye as now
And wel'come death more mercifull then thou.

37   To veiw thy beauty well, if thou be wise,
Come not to gaze upon this glass of thyne
But come and looke upon these eyes of myne,
Where thou shalt see thy true resemblance twyce,
Or if thou thinkes that thou profaines thy eyes
When on my wretched eyes they daigne to shyne,
Looke on my heart wherein, as in a shryne,
The lively picture of thy beauty lyes,
Or if thy harmeless modesty thinkes shame
To gaze upon the horrours of my heart,
Come read those lynes and reading see in them
The trophies of thy beautie and my smart,
Or if to none of those thou'l daigne to come,
Weepe eyes, breake heart and you my verse be dumbe.

38   Faire famous flood, which sometyme did devyde
But now conjoynes two diadems in one,
Suspend thy pace and some more softly slyde;
Since wee have made the trinchman of our mone
And since non's left but thy report alone
To show the world our captaines last farewell
That courtesye I knowe when wee are gon
Perhapps your lord the sea will it reveale
And you againe the same will not conceale

---

trinchman spokesman   *mone* complaint

But straight proclaim't through all his bremish bounds
Till his high tydes these flowing tydeings tell
And soon will send them with his murmering sounds
To that religious place, whose stately walls
Does keepe the heart which all our hearts inthralls.

39   Forsaken of all comforts but these two,
My faggott and my pipe, I sitt and muse
On all my crosses and almost accuse
The heavens for dealing with me as they doe.
Then hope steps in and, with a smyling brow,
Such chearfull expectations doth infuse
As makes me think ere long I cannot chuse
But be some Grandie, whatsoever I'm now.
But haveing spent my pype, I then perceive
That hopes and dreames are couzens, both deceive.
Then make I this conclusion in my minde,
Its all one thing, both tends unto one scope
To live upon tobacco and on hope,
The ones but smoake, the other is but winde.

William Drummond

40   I know that all beneath the moone decayes,
And what by mortalles in this world is brought,
In Times great periods shall returne to nought,
That fairest states have fatall nights and dayes;
I know how all the Muses heavenly layes,
With toyle of spright which are so dearely bought,
As idle sounds of few, or none, are sought
And that nought lighter is than airie praise.
I know fraile Beautie like the purple flowre,
To which one morne oft birth and death affords,
That Love a jarring is of mindes accords,
Where Sense and Will invassall Reasons power:
Know what I list, this all can not mee move,
But that (ô mee!) I both must write and love.

---

bremish raging   *couzens* frauds   *invassal* usurp

41 Sleepe, silence child, sweet father of soft rest,
   Prince whose approach peace to all mortalls brings,
   Indifferent host to shepheards and to kings,
   Sole comforter of minds with griefe opprest,
   Loe, by thy charming rod all breathing things
   Lie slumbring, with forgetfulnesse possest,
   And yet o're me to spred thy drowsie wings
   Thou spares (alas) who cannot be thy guest.
   Since I am thine, O come, but with that face
   To inward light which thou art wont to show,
   With fained solace ease a true felt woe,
   Or if, deafe God, thou doe denie that grace,
   Come as thou wilt, and what thou wilt bequeath.
   I long to kisse the image of my death.

42 Slide soft faire Forth, and make a christall plaine,
   Cut your white lockes, and on your foamie face
   Let not a wrinckle bee, when you embrace
   The boat that Earths Perfections doth containe.
   Windes wonder, and through wondring holde your peace,
   Or if that yee your hearts cannot restraine
   From sending sighes, mov'd by a lovers case,
   Sigh, and in her faire haire your selves enchaine:
   Or take these sighes which absence makes arise
   From mine oppressed brest and wave the sailes,
   Or some sweet breath new brought from Paradise:
   Flouds seeme to smile, love o're the winds prevailes,
   And yet hudge waves arise, the cause is this,
   The ocean strives with Forth the boate to kisse.

43 As in a duskie and tempestuous night,
   A starre is wont to spreade her lockes of gold,
   And while her pleasant rayes abroad are roll'd,
   Some spitefull cloude doth robbe us of her sight:
   (Faire soule) in this black age so shin'd thou bright,
   And made all eyes with wonder thee beholde,
   Till uglie Death depriving us of light,
   In his grimme mistie armes thee did enfolde.
   Who more shall vaunt true beautie heere to see?
   What hope doth more in any heart remaine,

That such perfections shall his reason raine?
If beautie with thee borne too died with thee?
World, plaine no more of love, nor count his harmes,
With his pale trophees Death hath hung his armes.

44   Runne (sheepheards) run, where Bethleme blest appeares,
Wee bring the best of newes, bee not dismay'd,
A saviour there is borne, more olde than yeares,
Amidst heavens rolling hights this earth who stay'd;
In a poor cotage inn'd, a virgine maide,
A weakling did him beare, who all upbeares,
There is hee poorelie swadl'd in manger lai'd,
To whom too narrow swadlings are our spheares:
Runne (sheepheards) runne, and solemnize his birth,
This is that night, no, day growne great with blisse,
In which the power of Sathan broken is,
In heaven bee glorie, peace unto the earth.
Thus singing through the aire the angels swame,
And cope of starres re-echoed the same.

45   "These eyes (deare Lord) once brandons of desire,
Fraile scoutes betraying what they had to keepe,
Which their owne heart, than others set on fire,
Their traitrous blacke before thee heere out-weepe:
These lockes, of blushing deedes the faire attire,
Smooth-frizled waves, sad shelfes which shadow deepe,
Soule-stinging serpents in gilt curles which creepe,
To touch thy sacred feete doe now aspire.
In seas of care behold a sinking barke,
By windes of sharpe remorse unto thee driven;
O let mee not expos'd be Ruines marke,
My faults confest (Lord) say they are forgiven."
Thus sigh'd to Jesus the Bethanian faire,
His teare-wet feete still drying with her haire.

46   Why (worldlings) do ye trust fraile honours dreams
And leane to guilted glories, which decay?
Why doe yee toyle to registrate your names
On ycie pillars, which soone melt away?

---

raine rule   *plaine* complain   *brandons* torches

True honour is not heere, that place it clames,
Where black-brow'd night doth not exile the day,
Nor no farre-shining lamp dives in the sea,
But an eternall sunne spreades lasting beames:
There it attendeth you, where spotlesse bands
Of spirits stand gazing on their soveraigne blisse,
Where yeeres not hold it in their canckring hands,
But who once noble, ever noble is.
Looke home, lest hee your weakned wit make thrall,
Who Edens foolish gardner earst made fall.

Sir William Mure

47   O three times happie, if the day of grace
In my darke soule did (though but dimly) dawne,
If to my strugling thoughts proclamd were peace,
If from mine eyes the vaile of darknesse drawne,
If once the seed of true repentance sawne
Made gushing streames leave furrowes on my face;
Sinnes menstruous rags in pure transparent laune
Were chang't, O then how happie were my cace!
So darknesse paths no more my feete should trace,
So ever on a quyet conscience feast
Repentance planted so should vice displace,
So clenst from sinne, sinne's filth I should detest!
Grace, light, repentance, inward peace I crave,
Grant these, good Lord, for mee thy selfe who gave.

48   Jerusalem is of her freedome spoil'd,
Orders of mens devising there bee plac'd:
True Christ is bound, thief Barrabas assoild,
Esau much praised, Jacob much disgracd.
The heritage of God is all defacd,
Formalities to substance are preferd:
Lawes are imposd grievous to bee embracd,
Earths fatnesse upon Judas is conferd.
Eye weep, heart groan, black birds my mirth have mard,
Moon hath no light, the sun his beames withdraweth:
The mouth of godly Zephanie is bard
Because the truth in honestie hee showeth.
Fountains of life, which make Gods citie glad,
Are fild with earth, clear springs can not bee had.

assoil absolved

Hugh Barclay

49   My best belovit brother of the craft,
God if ye knew the stait that I am in!
Thocht ye be deif, I know ye ar not daft
Bot kynd aneugh to any of your kin.
If ye bot saw me in this winter win
With old bogogers hotching on a sped,
Draiglit in dirt, whylis wat evin to the [skin]
I trow thair suld be tears or we twa shed.
Bot maist of all, that hes my bailis bred
To heir how ye on that syde of the m[ure]
Birlis at the vyne, and blythlie gois to [bed],
Forgetting me, pure pleuman, I am sure.
So, sillie I, opprest with barmie jugg[is],
Invyis your state that's pouing Bacchus [luggis].

Mark Alexander Boyd

50   Fra banc to banc, fra wod to wod, I rin
Ourhailit with my feble fantasie,
Lyc til a leif that fallis from a trie
Or til a reid ourblawin with the wind.
Twa gods gyds me; the ane of tham is blind,
Ye, and a bairn brocht up in vanitie;
The nixt a wyf ingenrit of the se
And lichter nor a dauphin with hir fin.
Unhappie is the man for evirmaire
That teils the sand and sawis in the aire;
Bot twyse unhappier is he, I lairn,
That feidis in his hairt a mad desyre
And follows on a woman throw the fyre,
Led be a blind and teichit be a bairn.

---

win wind   *bogogers* leggings   *hotching* jerking   *sped* spade
whylis sometimes   *bailis* sorrows   *m[ure]* moor   *birlis* carouses
barmie jugg[is] frothy jugs   *invyis* envies   *pouing* pulling   *luggis* ears
ourhailit overcome   *bairn* child   *teils* tills   *teichit* taught

NOTES

(Double numbers, separated by a full stop, indicate, for the lyrics, first the verse and then the line; for the sonnets, first the sonnet, then the line.)

Anonymous

Hay Trix
Text: H. Charteris, *Ane Compendious Buik of Godlie Psalmes and Spirituall Sangis* (Edinburgh), 1576

1.7 Charteris: 'Hay trix, tryme go trix, under the grene, etc.' I follow the expansion suggested by J. and W. MacQueen in *A Choice of Scottish Verse 1470-1570* (London, 1972), p. 206.
2.5 'bot lardounis'. Meaning uncertain, but 'lardine' was an inferior substitute for lard and the sense may have generalised.
4 Refers to the various orders of friars, although Jacobins and Dominicans are really the same. Cordeliers are the Franciscan Observantines, who wore a knotted cord round their waists.
9.1 'Scotlandwell . . . Faill'. Scotlandwell is in Kinross and Faill in Ayrshire. Both were houses of the Red Friars. See D. E. Easson, *Medieval Religious Houses, Scotland* (London, 1957), pp. 90-5.
11.3 'The Congregatioun'. Specific reference to the group called the Congregation of Christ, who vowed in 1557 to support Protestantism. Most of their aims were achieved in the next three years.

Sir Richard Maitland
Text: *Maitland Folio MS*

Satire on the Age

1 Maitland, probably writing in the early 1560s, looks back rather wistfully to the Scotland of his youth prior to the economic, religious and social changes of the Reformation. See Brother Kenneth, 'The Popular Literature of the Reformation', in D. McRoberts, *Essays on the Scottish Reformation* (Glasgow, 1962).
6.1 'And we hald nother yule nor pace'. Two of the major Catholic festivals are no longer observed.
6.4 'We gar our landis doubill pay', and cf. 5.3. During the 1560s complaints of rack-renting, exorbitant rent augmentation and unfair eviction were common. See G. Donaldson, *James V-James VII* (Edinburgh, 1965), pp. 114-15 and 239-40.

8.5 'Thay had lang formes quhair we have stulis'. The corporate con-
viviality of the pre-Reformation banquet is set against the stool as an
image of solitude. There may be a particular association with the 'stool of
repentance'.

10.5 'bayth the court and sessioun'. The MS alteration from 'kirk' to
'court' makes better sense.

Aganis the Theivis of Liddisdaill

1.1 'Off Liddisdaill the commoun thevis'. The reference is to the border
reivers living in the valley of the Liddel Water near Langholm. Much
thieving, often with the knowing connivance of the nobility, went on
on both sides of the border. Maitland was himself appointed one of the
commissioners for the border area. See T. I. Rae, *The Administration of
the Scottish Frontier 1513-1603* (Edinburgh, 1966).

4.2 'Ettrik forrest and Lauderdaill'. The area round the Ettrick Water
south of Selkirk and the valley of the Leader Water in the Lauder/Earlston
region.

4.3 'Now ar thai gane in Lowthiane'. The reivers are moving north into
the Lothians and so closer to Maitland himself.

6.1 'blak maile'. A yearly sum paid by farmers in the borders to a
chieftain, who undertook to make good any losses caused by reiving.

7.3 'Will of the Lais, Hab of the Schais'. Nicknames of specific reivers
in the area. See R. B. Armstrong, *The History of Liddesdale* (Edinburgh,
1883), pp. 78-9.

Solace in Age

1.2 'And thevis hes done my rowmes range'. A reference to the 1570
raid on his own property at Blyth.

1.4 'Change' is a marginal alteration; orig. 'chynge'.

9 The 'weir' referred to is still, on one level, the sexual war with puns
on 'hors', 'harnes', 'speir', and 'hoisting geir'.

Robert Sempill

The Ballat maid upoun Margret Fleming
Text: *Bannatyne MS*

3.4 'To stop hir hoilis laich in the howiss'. The pun depends on 'howiss'
meaning both 'the holds of a ship' and 'legs'.

5.7 'nocht'. Orig. 'nochthing', but 'hing' deleted in MS.

5.8 A marginal addition in a later hand reads 'to Ioh' carmichaell'.

7.5 'about'. MS 'a bowt'.

8.4 'Scho will be kittill of hir dok'. The secondary meaning is 'her rump
will be easily stimulated'.

Alexander Montgomerie

The Cherrie and the Slae
Text: *Wreittoun*, 1636 (here abbreviated *Wr*). See Introduction (pages 17-21 for discussion of the textual problems involved. Some readings from Waldegrave II (*WII*) have been introduced. Ramsay's *Evergreen* (*E*) edition has been regarded as of lesser authority

1   Progne and Philomela were sisters, the former being married to King Tereus of Trace. He raped Philomela and cut out her tongue but she told the story in a tapestry. Later Progne was turned into a swallow and Philomela into a nightingale.
2.4 'jargoun of': *Wr* 'largoun or'; *E* 'jargoun or'.
2.10 'And Echo answered . . .' Echo was a tree nymph, who pined and died for love of Narcissus. Nemesis punished Narcissus for his lack of feeling by making him fall in love with his own image.
4.5 'Apollos paramours'. Apollo was represented as a young man of ideal beauty. He became amorously involved with Daphne, Coronis, Cyrene and others.
4.10 'Cled'. The *WII* reading gives a better rhyme than *Wr*'s 'clad'.
7.7 'the C-sol-fa-uth cleife'. Staff notation. So called after certain syllables in a hymn by the eighth-century Lombard Paulus Diaconus.
8   The *WII* version of this stanza appears in James VI's *Reulis and Cautelis* as an example of 'cuttit and brokin verse'.
8.6 'natures chappel clarks'. A common formula for birds.
12.4 'As Icarus with borrowed flight . . .' Icarus, son of Daedalus, was given waxen wings, which melted as he approached the sun. He became a type of ignorant aspiration.
12.7 'double dart'. The arrows of Cupid could produce love or aversion.
13.7 'As foolish Phaeton'. Apollo's son whose failure to guide his father's chariot properly set the world on fire.
14.4 'Too late I heard the swallow preach'. In one of Aesop's Fables the swallow wisely counselled the other birds but was ignored. See Henryson's 'The Preiching of the Swallow'.
15.6 'As Reason quite miskens'. The problem of whether Reason or Will was the ruling faculty was a central concern of the patristic philosophers. In particular Aquinas argued for the primacy of Reason and Scotus for Will. See F. Copleston, *A History of Philosophy* Vol. 2 (London, 1959). In *The Cherrie and the Slae* Montgomerie appears to side with the Thomist position.
18.11 'Like Dido'. Dido was the reputed founder of Carthage. In Virgil's *Aeneid* she falls in love with Aeneas and kills herself after his departure for Italy.

19.7 and 9 'devorit . . . smor it'. *WII* 'devorit . . . smorit'; *Wr* 'devourde . . . smoorde'. The *WII* reading gives better sense and a more exact rhyme.

20.2 'an atomie'. *Wr* 'Anatomie'; *WII* 'ane atomie'.

24.5 'glansing'. *Wr* omits. *WII* has 'glansing' and clearly the metre demands this.

24.12 'as Dornick champe'. A type of cloth embroidered with flowers or figures.

25.7 'I calde to minde how Daphne did . . .' Daphne was turned into a laurel when overtaken by the amorous Apollo. Ovid, *Metamorphoses*, I, 452–567.

30.9 'Be not a novice of that nunnes . . .' I have been unable to trace the source of this allusion.

31.9 and 12 'Atropus' and 'Clotho'. Respectively the Fates governing death and birth.

32.1 'All ou'rs are repute to be vice'. The doctrine of the harmonious mean was central to classical thought and championed in particular by Pythagoras and Horace. It was also central to James VI's philosophical and political theories.

33.1 'thrist'. *WII* reading. *Wr* 'thirst' does not give an exact rhyme.

36 Proverbs play a large part in this stanza and in Montgomerie's verse generally. In the Renaissance they were an important figure in rhetorical training and were held to represent in pithy form the crystallised experience of mankind.

39.10 'spreit'. *WII* reading. *Wr* 'sprite' does not give an exact rhyme.

40.6 'The lurking serpent lyes'. Traditionally associated with the devil and sin. See Henryson, *Orpheus and Eurydice*, lines 441–4.

43.14 'yit'. *WII* reading. *Wr* 'yet' does not give an exact rhyme.

47.7 'Ye sell the baires skin on his back'. The equivalent modern proverb would be 'to count one's chickens before they are hatched'.

49.6 'To leade him all their lanes'. *WII* reading 'him' makes better sense than *Wr* 'them'.

51.1 'Goe, goe, we nothing doe'. *Wr* 'We doe nothing'; *WII* 'We naithing do'.

55.12 and 14 'conceal it . . . reveal it'. *Wr* 'concealde . . . reveald'; *WII* 'conceill . . . reveill'. *Wr* makes little sense as it stands but the form suggests anglicisation of the '-it' form of the past participle in Middle Scots. The printer probably mistook the infinitive + it for the Scots past participle and then anglicised.

59.3 'yit'. Gives exact rhyme. *Wr* 'yet'.

60.4 'Quoth Reason . . .' Reason's argument in this and the following stanzas depends on the presumption that it is man's rational faculty which separates him from the beasts and gives him at once greater potential and greater responsibilities.

62.10 'Take yee two asses eares . . .' Midas got his ears for misuse of the senses. He preferred Pan's music to that of Apollo. Ovid, *Metamorphoses*, XI, 178-9.

64.1 'Then Will, as angry as an ape'. Will's bestial reaction confirms Reason's argument.

65.5 'Yee'. *Wr* 'Yet'; *E* 'Ye'.

67.4 'a bony while'. Can mean either a long or a short time. The context suggests the former.

67.8 'mov'd'. *Wr* 'mo'vd'.

70.8 'spreit'. *WII* reading. *Wr* 'spirit' dislocates metre and does not give an exact rhyme.

70.11 'Thy punces, pronunces'. Methods of timing the pulse were first discovered in the late sixteenth century. Montgomerie is thus referring to a new diagnostic method.

71.3 and 6 'contraks . . . maks' *WII*. *Wr* 'contracts . . . makes' is an imperfect rhyme.

72.5 'The man that will not . . .' This proverb earlier appeared in Henryson's *Robene and Makyne*.

74.5 'ye gart them'. *WII* reading. *Wr* 'ye gart us' makes no obvious sense.

75.10 'That Danger lap the dyke' – i.e. fled and hid.

75.11 'Quoth Dreid'. *WII* reading. *Wr* 'Danger' does not provide the necessary internal rhyme. Almost certainly the compositor erroneously repeated 'Danger' from the line above.

76.5 'trow it'. *WII* reading. *Wr* 'trowit'.

78.4 'yit'. *Wr* 'yet' does not provide an exact rhyme. Also see 87.6 and 108.5.

79.9 'In your owne bow you are ou'rshot'. You are beaten with your own weapon.

81.4 'For ay since Adam and since Eve'. Experience cunningly equates his opponent's arguments with those of the devil.

83.5 'a plack'. A small coin, of very little value.

85.6 'And fleets'. Grammatically correct, this reading was erroneously altered to 'fleet' by Ramsay in *E*.

90.2 'Yet Courage could not overcome'. The understood subject is the 'hee' of 90.1.

94.4 'bygone'. *Wr* 'bygones'.

98.13 'Then urge him to purge him'. Montgomerie returns to the medical metaphor used in Stanzas 70, 71. Purging, or relieving the body by evacuation, was thought to purify it and to relieve fever.

102.6 'Ou'r rackles may repent'. A return to the theme of the 'media via', already broached in Stanza 32.

105.12 'baith'. *Wr* 'both'. The Scots form is needed for an exact rhyme.

106.8 'The gods of both these parts'. Might refer either to the gods of the upper and nether regions or to the gods supporting the respective sides of the debate.

107.13 'restis'. *Wr* 'rest is.'

109.3 'That we have nam'd no guide'. Cf *Piers Plowman*, Passus VI, 'This were a wikked way but whoso hadde a gyde'. Reason's choice of Wit (that is, practical wisdom) suggests that the cherry is not of the highest spiritual significance. Wit always drops out before the final stages of an ultimate theological quest.

110 Many critics have tried to give an exact location to the quest. The most plausible solution is A. A. MacDonald's suggestion of a spot near the confluence of the Rivers Tarff and Don. A short distance up the Dee beyond the bridge carrying the Kirkcudbright road there is the requisite ford, the sheer-faced cliff and a pool known as the Linn Pool. Certainty is, however, impossible and the problem largely irrelevant to the meaning of the poem.

113.10 'The fruite for ripnes fell'. The dreamer gains the cherry through God's grace, but the falling of the cherry itself illustrates an important feature of grace. It is, according to Augustine and Aquinas, ready for man at all times. Although he cannot attain it unaided, only his blindness prevents this gift from being given to him. Now that the dreamer is knowledgeable, the cherry falls. See Introduction, page 20.

Sweit Hairt rejoss in Mynd
Text: *Laing III, 447*

The presence of this lyric in a MS containing some of Montgomerie's work and certain stylistic similarities are the main reasons for attributing it to him. It should perhaps more strictly be regarded as an Anonymous poem.

Quhill as with Whyt and Nimble Hand
Text: *Drummond MS*

A Description of Tyme
Text: *Drummond MS*

1.3 'Sho hes no hold to hold hir by bot ane'. The reference is to the goddess Occasio, who had long hair in front to prevent recognition and was bald behind to prevent mortals seizing her.

Lyk as the Dum Solsequium
Text: *Drummond MS*

This lyric appears in nearly all the editions of *The Cherrie and the Slae* and is usually entitled 'The Solsequium'. The music was printed in *Cantus, Songs and Fancies* (Aberdeen, 1662). The omissions in the Drummond MS, indicated by square brackets, have been supplied from the Bannatyne MS version.

1.9 'Till folish Phaeton ryse'. See note on *The Cherrie and the Slae*, 13.7 (page 161). Phaeton is often depicted as a Sun God in Homer and Hesiod.

4.3 'Apollo stay' – i.e. let day continue.

4.5 and 6 'Of me thou mak/Thy zodiak' – i.e. he asks the sun to submit to his control. The zodiac is an imaginary belt in the heavens through which the ecliptic passes. It was believed to control the movements of sun, moon and planets.

4.15 'Sen "primum mobile" . . .' The tenth sphere of the Ptolemaic system. It carries all the other spheres.

Away, Vane World
Text: *Drummond MS*

Hay, now the Day Dawis
Text: *Drummond MS*

A folk song, adapted by Montgomerie and set to the tune 'Hey tuttie taittie'. Gavin Douglas refers to this song in the Prologue to Book VIII of *Eneados*. The song originated about 1500, being one of a collection addressed to Elizabeth, daughter of Edward IV. The MS often omits 'i' when it seems metrically necessary. In my text these 'i's' have been introduced.

John Stewart of Baldynneis

Roland Furious

Roland (Orlando), the hero of the epic, is searching for his enemy Mandricard (Mandricardo) whose horse ran off during their conflict. His quest is to bring him by chance to the grove where his lady Angelique (Angelica) had earlier discovered her love for the young Moor, Medor (Medoro). This canto marks Roland's fall from the heights of power into despair and madness. See R. D. S. Jack, *The Italian Influence on Scottish Literature* (Edinburgh, 1972), pp. 57-71.

Text: *MS National Library of Scotland Adv. 19.2.6*

Line 3: 'Ramnusia' – i.e. the girl from Rhamnus and hence Nemesis, the avenger. Rhamnus was a town in northern Attica, famed for its statue of Nemesis.

9: 'Wold god, Bocace mycht in my place repair'. Stewart is thinking primarily of the *De Casibus Virorum Illustrium* and the *De Claris Mulieribus*. These collections deal largely with men and women who were cast down by Fortune. Chaucer's *Monk's Tale* is another probable influence.

22: 'my Prence'. James VI, to whom the MS was presented.

23: 'the gowldin graine' – i.e. the golden bough of knowledge, which enabled Aeneas to explore the Nether World in *Aeneid* Book VI. In *Eneados* Douglas also refers to 'this goldin grane'.

32: 'Nabuchodonosors great decay'. Nebuchadnezzar was King of Babylon from 604–561 BC. Under his rule the kingdom reached its zenith of power. His final degradation into bestialism is traced in Daniel 4, verse 33.

33: 'The monarck Ninus that in preson lay'. In Greek myth, Ninus was the founder of Nineveh and conqueror of Western Asia. His wife Semiramis persuaded him to make her sole ruler for five days during which time she imprisoned and murdered him.

35: 'The puissant Cyrus, King of Perse . . .' According to Herodotus, Cyrus overthrew but spared the life of Croesus, king of Lydia. He was finally defeated by Tomyris, queen of the Massagetae, who placed his head in a skin filled with human blood.

37: 'Great Alexander poysand but remeed'. Alexander actually died of fever. Plutarch discounts as mere fables the theories that he was poisoned either by Olympias or Antipater.

38: 'Nor mychtie Cesar, quho was schortlie slaine'. Julius Caesar was slain by a band of those who were offended by his increasingly autocratic attitudes. The leaders of the conspiracy were Marcus Brutus and Caius Cassius.

46: 'Thy hautie wavering hairis . . . The reference is to Fortune as Occasio. See note on 'A Description of Tyme', 1.3 (page 164).

50–6: 'Dame Indiscreit I sute of the no grace . . .' This may be a veiled reference to Stewart's own situation and in particular to the Redcastle affair: see M. P. McDiarmid, 'John Stewart of Baldynneis', *Scottish Historical Review*, XXIX, 52–63.

59: 'Great Bajacet that Turk . . .' Bajazet I, a sultan of the Ottoman Empire, was defeated by Timur Khan (or Tamburlaine) in 1402 near Ancora. Bajazet's subsequent imprisonment is dramatically presented by Marlowe in *Tamburlaine the Great*, Part I.

65: 'that potent King of France . . .' Henry II, killed in 1559 during a tournament held to celebrate the marriage of his daughter.

Line 69: 'King Alexander is exemple meit'. Alexander III, king of Scotland, died 19 March 1286. After attending a late conference at Edinburgh Castle, he rode back to Kinghorn to rejoin his queen. On the way his horse stumbled over a cliff, throwing him to his death.

84: 'Bot as Pompey or hardie Hanniball'. Pompey was a Roman general whose great power was finally crushed at Pharsalia in 48 BC. He was assassinated while seeking sanctuary in Egypt. Hannibal was a Carthaginian general, who greatly extended that country's power. He was finally driven into exile by the Romans and poisoned himself in 182 BC.

86: 'The strong, redouttit, dochtie Darius'. Darius III, ruler of Persia in the fourth century BC, saw his power crumble before Alexander. He fled after the Battle of Issus (333 BC), leaving his family in enemy hands. Later his forces were routed by Alexander and he was murdered by his Bactrian satrap, Bessus.

91: 'as Arius'. Arius was a Christian heresiarch, who was driven into exile by the Nicene Council. He founded Arianism and died an excommunicate in 336.

101: 'Queine Semerame thou lang did welthie leed'. See note on line 33. She was wife of Ninus and herself a conqueror on the grand scale. Boccaccio places her second after Eve in his list of famous women. She was finally defeated by King Stabrobates in a battle on the banks of the Indus.

105: 'Dame Panthasile'. Also mentioned in Boccaccio's *De Claris Mulieribus*. She was a queen of the Amazons, who became infatuated with Hector and died in a battle against the Greeks.

113: 'Zenobia'. Queen of Palmyra in the third century AD. She extended her territories from Egypt to the Bosphorus, but was crushed by the Emperor Aurelian in 272 after having rebelled against Rome.

150: 'Nor Hector, traillit at Achylles steid'. In Homer, Hector is the eldest son of the Trojan king Priam and chief warrior of Troy. The Greek hero Achilles finally slays him and drags his body round the walls of Troy. It is, however, preserved by Apollo and Aphrodite.

160: 'At last in schersing Mandricard so fell'. Mandricardo came to avenge himself on Orlando for killing his father Agricane. At this point, the two foes have been separated in battle and Orlando is searching for his opponent in order to begin hostilities again.

176: 'Quhair scho and Medor wont was to remaine'. Medoro is a young Moor of humble rank, who followed Prince Dardinello into the French wars and won the love of Angelica.

253: 'And oft he red it . . .' – i.e. he tried to extract a false meaning from the obvious one.

294: 'Bridedor' – lit. golden bridle. Orlando's horse.

Line 299: 'Till his palle sister Phebe giffing place'. The introduction of the word 'Phebe' into this line suggests that Stewart was working from Jean Martin's French prose version of the *Orlando Furioso*. See Introduction, page 24.

325: 'The wofull wreat'. The poems and other memorials of love, which Medoro had carved or written all over the lovers' retreat. *Orlando Furioso* Canto 23, Stanzas 129, 130.

400: 'As quhan ane pastor schersing eisment lyis'. Elaborate homeric similes play an important part in this poem. Cf 559 ff.

412: 'Blasphems the heavens . . .' Although his blasphemy is here expressed in terms of the pagan gods, Orlando's madness is firmly established by Stewart as a symptom of the hero's wilful turning away from the Christian God. This is made much more explicit in Canto XII of *Roland Furious* than in Ariosto.

443: 'This liquor brycht Is no moir teirs . . .' Cf. the grief of Stewart's hero with that of Hieronimo in Act 3 of Kyd's *Spanish Tragedy*. 'O eyes! no eyes, but fountains fraught with tears . . .' The origin of this motif may be Sannazaro's sonnet, 'O vita, vita non, ma vivo affanno'.

468: 'His dame ingrait' – i.e. Angelica.

486: 'dochtie Durandal'. Orlando's sword.

613: 'bot be the ring'. Angelica's ring could make her invisible.

625: 'For imperfyt and tedius I confes . . .' In the final passage of this Canto, Stewart explains some of the methods lying behind his 'Abbregement'. In particular he tries to convert Ariosto's expansive, episodic form into a tighter pattern governed by thematic parallels.

Of Ane Symmer Hous

Text: *MS National Library of Scotland Adv. 19.2.6*

2.1 'Quhat Nymphe or Dian sall posses the now'. The poet wonders whether the bower is now the scene of sensual or chaste pursuits.

Alexander Hume

Of the Day Estivall

This poem with its precise and imaginative description of nature is a remarkable phenomenon for this period. It looks back to the descriptive prologues of Gavin Douglas' *Eneados* (particularly Book XII) and forward to Thomson's *Seasons*.

Text: Waldegrave, *Hymnes or Sacred Songs*, 1599. The MS version in the National Library of Scotland is editorially of little consequence.

1.1 'O perfite light . . .' The God of Genesis. Hume introduces Nature, not as an end in itself but as a means of establishing God's glory.

4.3 'like natures clerks'. A common formula for birds. Cf. *C and S* 8.6 and Note.

5.4 'Them selves in house to hide'. Waldegrave reading. As this makes reasonable sense, I am not convinced that the usual editorial emendation to 'howis' = hollows, lairs, is justified.

6.4 'As lyons to their den'. Waldegrave 'And lyons . . .' makes little sense.

11 This stanza with its reference to vines is often used as an argument that Hume is thinking of France, where he spent a number of years. But Britain had vines, too, as Bede and later Gavin Douglas remind us. More important, surely, is the association with the Parable of the Vineyard and the image of orderly Christian endeavour on the field of life.

14.3 'The glansing phains'. The Waldegrave reading 'thains' makes little sense. 'Wains' = 'dwellings' has been suggested as a solution but the context seems to call for 'phains' or 'vanes of a window'.

28.3 'Bot be the high and haly On . . .' Usually the pagan gods were used in the Renaissance as a useful poetic metaphor for the Christian God. [See J. Seznec, *The Survival of the Pagan Gods* (New York, 1961).] Hume, a man of the Reformation, insists on distinguishing between the two.

32.3 'made the beare'. Waldegrave has 'made thee beare'. Most editors amend to 'made the beir', but 'beare' = 'noise' was an acceptable alternative form at that time.

37.3 'the reamand London beare'. Waldegrave has 'the rime, and London beare', which makes no sense.

44.3 'Ilk labourer'. Waldegrave has 'Quhilk labourer'.

58 The poem ends as it began with a direct reference to God. The Vineyard parable is again evoked, while there is, perhaps, an echo of Psalm 104, verse 23: 'Man goeth forth unto his work and to his labour until the evening.'

Sir Robert Ayton

Ayton's poems present a tricky editorial problem. Both Laing MS III 436 (Edinburgh University) and B. Museum Add. MS 10308 have high authority. The latter may well be a later, anglicised reworking of the texts presented in Laing, although certainty is not possible. (See C. B. Gullans, New Poems by Sir Robert Ayton', *Modern Language Review*, LV, 162–4.) I have used Laing as copy in cases where versions from both MSS exist and B. Museum Add. 10308 elsewhere. This permits an interesting comparison between 'Scots' and 'anglicised' versions of work by the same author. See Helena M. Shire, *Song, Dance and Poetry of the Court of Scotland under King James VI* (Cambridge, 1969), pp. 215–54.

To his Coy Mistres
Text: *Laing MS III, 436*

The poem should be compared with Montgomerie's 'Love, if thou list, I pray the let me leiv'. (*Poems*, ed. Cranstoun, p. 161.)
Line 5: 'Too'. Ed. MS reads 'two'.
     7: 'hotter'. I have followed Gullans' emendation. MS reads 'better'.

The Shiphird Thirsis longed to die
Text: *Laing MS III, 436*

Line 1: 'The shiphird Thirsis longed to die'. 'Die' is throughout used as a sexual pun.
     4: 'When'. Add. 10308. The Laing reading, 'Whom', is probably an example of scribal anticipation.

Lov's like a Game at Irish
Text: *British Museum Additional MS 10308*

A witty piece of sexual double-entendre based on a single, extended conceit. It is in the same tradition as 'The Ballat maid upoun Margret Fleming' and Stewart's 'hostess' sonnets.
Line 1: 'Lov's like a game at Irish'. Irish is a game resembling backgammon.

An Epigram and *Shall Feare to seeme Untrue*
Text: Both *British Museum Additional MS 10308*

William Drummond

A Dedale of my Death
Text: *Poems* (Edinburgh), 1616

Line 1: 'A Dedale of my death'. The poem is a fairly close translation of Guarini's 'Fabro dela mia morte'. Daedalus, son of Metion, was a mythical Greek figure representing all handiwork. He was imprisoned in his own maze by Minos and is thus a fitting image for selfwrought destruction.
     2: 'that subtile worme' – i.e. the Devil.

Like the Idalian Queene
Text: *Poems* (Edinburgh), 1616

Line 1: 'the Idalian queene'. Venus, to whom the Cypriot town of Idalium was sacred.
     14: 'A hyacinth I wisht mee in her hand'. There is probably an intended association with Hyacinthus, the beautiful youth beloved by Apollo and Zephyrus. The poet wishes he could also inspire love.

A Lovers Prayer and *The Qualitie of a Kisse*
Text: *Poems* (Edinburgh), 1616

Upon a Glasse
Text: *Poems* (Edinburgh), 1616

Lines 13 and 14: 'No planets . . . amber haire'. This type of parallel construction was known as underwriting. It was also much practised by Ayton and Stewart of Baldynneis.

It was the Time when to our Northerne Pole
Text: *Poems* (Edinburgh), 1616

The passage cited is the introduction to one of Drummond's longer dream vision poems. For the full text, see L. E. Kastner, *The Poetical Works of Drummond of Hawthornden* (Edinburgh, 1913), I, 9-16.
Line 11: 'By Oras flowrie bancks'. The Ore or Ore Water is in Fife. Drummond is reputed to have loved a Miss Euphemia Cunningham, who lived near this river. See, however, R. H. MacDonald, 'Drummond of Hawthornden, Miss Euphemia Kyninghame and the Poems', *Modern Language Review*, LX, 494-9.
    12: 'to old Meander'. A river in Phrygia, noted for its winding course.
    13: 'a floud more worthie fame . . .' Drummond suggests that the Ore is more worthy of fame than the Po.
    30: 'This little Arden might Elysium be'. Elysium was the abode of the blessed. Arden is here used in the same sense of wooded retreat as in *As You Like It*. Originally, in Thomas Lodge's story of Rosalynde, it had represented the Ardennes region of France.
    32: 'And Acidalias queene'. Venus, who used to bathe with the Graces in the well Acidalius.
    55: 'Here Adon blush't and Clitia all amazed'. Adon = the rose. According to Bion, *Idyll* I, the rose sprang from the blood of Adonis. Clitia = the heliotrope. Ovid relates how Clitia, daughter of Oceanus, was changed into this flower (*Metamorphoses*, IV, 6).
    56: 'with him who in the fountaine gazed' – i.e. Narcissus.
    57: 'The Amaranthus smyl'd and that sweet boy'. The Amaranthus is associated with the genus which includes Prince's Feather, but poetically it is usually regarded as an imaginary flower, which never fades. 'That sweet boy' is Hyacinthus.

The Country Maid
Text: *Hawthornden MS X*

A Jest
Text: *Poems* (Edinburgh), 1616

Great God, whom Wee with Humble Thoughts Adore
Text: *Flowres of Sion* (Edinburgh), 1630. An earlier version appears in *Poems* (Edinburgh), 1616

Line 4: 'Archangells serve, and Seraphines doe sing'. Two of the nine angelic orders. Usually the seraphim were regarded as the highest rank and archangels the eighth.

9 and 10: 'Ah! spare . . . lawes rebell'. Cf. 'A Dedale of my death', lines 2, 3.

15: 'Passe shall this world . . .' The reference is to the Day of Judgment and the anticipated union of the four daughters of God – Justice, Mercy, Truth and Peace.

48: 'our first parents pride'. Adam and Eve's aspiration to be as God, through eating the forbidden fruit in Eden.

Sir William Mure

The Cry of Blood and of a Broken Covenant
Text: *1650 edition*

This is the opening of the poem. For the full text, see *The Works of Sir William Mure*, ed. W. Tough (Edinburgh, 1898), II, 33-52.

Line 1: 'What horrid actings . . .' Mure refers to the execution of Charles I. See R. D. S. Jack, 'Sir William Mure and the Covenant', *Records of the Scottish Church History Society*, XVIII, 1-14.

19 and 20: 'In trumpets . . . deeply drown'd'. Mure foresees that the Scots will fight on behalf of Charles II. Their forces were defeated by Cromwell at Dunbar, September 1650. See G. Donaldson, *James V–James VII* (Edinburgh, 1965), pp. 340-1.

Robert Sempill of Beltrees

The Life and Death of Habbie Simson
Text: Watson's *Choice Collection*, 1706. Occasional readings from the 1689 broadside versions (*B*) in the National Library of Scotland have been introduced

1.1 'Kilbarchan'. A small village in Renfrewshire.

2.2 'Hunts Up'. Watson reads 'hunt up'. Clearly the reference is to the well-known folk tune, and therefore the reading of *B* has been adopted.

4.2 'At Beltan and Saint Barchan's feast'. Beltane was the ancient Celtic festival held at the start of May. St Barchan was an Irish bishop, who worked near Stirling.

8.1 'a wail'd wight-man'. Watson has 'weil'd Wight-man', which makes dubious sense. *B*'s reading has been adopted.

10.2 'With Kittock hinging at his side'. 'Kittock' refers to Habbies' dirk named after Colla Ciotach (i.e. MacDonald of Colonsay).

12.3 'Borcheugh'. *B* has 'Barheugh'.

13 This stanza does not appear in *B*. See the discussion by G. Ross Roy in his Introduction to *The Life and Death of the Piper of Kilbarchan* (Edinburgh, 1970).

A detailed discussion of the many complex allusions in this poem appears in Kenneth Buthlay's recent article 'Habbie Simson' in *Bards and Makars* (Glasgow, 1977).

The Sonnet

These sonnets have not been grouped chronologically but in the order which best represents the development of the genre in Scotland. James VI's contribution comes first as he was the prime populariser of the form. Stewart and Montgomerie were his major Castalian disciples, while Fowler's *Tarantula of Love* provides a useful 'bridge' to the later love sequences by Alexander, Murray and Craig. Ayton and Drummond mark the climax of this movement, while William Mure's collection provides a passionate Covenanting postscript. The individual sonnets by Hugh Barclay and Mark Alexander Boyd are among the finest of those composed by occasional practitioners in the genre. See R. Jack, *The Scottish Sonnet and Renaissance Poetry* (Ph.D. thesis, Edinburgh, 1968).

James VI
Text: *British Museum Additional MS 24195*

1 This sonnet is one of a short sequence addressed by the King to Anne of Denmark prior to their marriage.

1.6 'And as of female sexe like stiffe in will'. James had opposed excesses of flattery in his *Reulis and Cautelis*!

1.9 'Then happie monarch . . .' Fergus was the legendary first king of Scotland. The 'happie monarch' therefore is James himself.

1.10ff   A convenient conceit, suggesting that Anne combines the qualities of wisdom, chastity and beauty.

2.1 'crawling Vulcan'. An early Roman fire God, later identified with Hephaestus. He was born a cripple.

3 This sonnet is a skilful adaptation of Desportes' *Diane*, I, 5.

4 This and two other sonnets were almost certainly composed in 1593 and deal with an attempt by Earl Bothwell to seize the king. Bothwell succeeded in entering the king's bedroom, carrying an unsheathed sword in his hand, but the escapade failed.

John Stewart of Baldynneis
Text: *MS National Library of Scotland, Adv. 19.2.6*

5   This sonnet is based on Desportes' 'Cette fontaine est froide'.

5.2   'As brychtest christall cleir'. Desportes has 'semble parler d'amour' at the equivalent point in his poem. Stewart omits this and provides no equivalent in line 7 for 'soupirant amoureux'. As a result the amorous emphasis in the French sonnet disappears.

5.9   And Titan'. Usually the elder brother of Kronos, but sometimes, as here, used to refer to his grandson the Sun god.

7   This is the first of two sonnets united by the same bawdy, 'hostess' conceit. In the second, the 'hostess' delivers an even more cutting retort, culminating with the advice that her visitor take her 'bak chalmer' for his 'guckit nois'!

8   One of Stewart's virtuoso sonnets. It is an example of what Molinet calls *vers enchayenné*, in which 'la fin d'un mètre est pareil en voix au commencement de l'autre'. The Scottish poets of the later Renaissance were greatly influenced by the French Rhétoriqueurs.

9.1   'O silver hornit Diane . . .' Diana (the moon) loved the shepherd Endymion and put him to sleep so that she might come down each night to kiss him. Ovid, *Amores* I, xiii, 43, 4.

9.14   'my secreit luif synceir'. This appears to be the first Scottish sonnet which deals with the conventions of courtly love.

10.8   'ryche'. MS 'rythche.'

Alexander Montgomerie
Texts: Nos. 11–16, *Drummond MS*; No. 17, *Laing III, 447*

11   This sonnet is probably intended as a comment on the increasing persecution of Catholics in Scotland, their exclusion from high office and frequent imprisonment. Montgomerie, himself a Catholic, had experience of both.

11.6   'with symonie defyld'. This refers to the buying of positions in the church. See Acts 8, verses 18, 19.

12   Montgomerie was eventually deprived of his pension but only after losing a bitter court case. See Helena M. Shire, *Song, Dance and Poetry of the Court of Scotland under King James VI* (Cambridge, 1969). This flyting sonnet is addressed to M. J. Sharp, his advocate, after the outcome was known.

12.13   'A Turk that tint Tranent for the Tolbuith'. As the Court of Session met at that time in the Tolbooth, and as the evidence suggests that Sharp came from an East Lothian family, the point of this allusion seems to be that he left his home town (Tranent) to become an advocate. 'Turk' is merely an alliterative convenience, having the force of 'scoundrel'. I am grateful to Professor Gordon Donaldson and to Mr. M. P. McDiarmid for advice on this tricky point.

12.14 'he is sharpe forsuith'. A pun on the advocate's name.

13 The sonnet is addressed to Robert Hudson, one of two English poets resident at James's court. After Montgomerie's fall from favour, due to his complicity in Catholic undertakings, Hudson took his place as 'maister poete'. Montgomerie may be pleading with his successor to intercede with the king on his behalf.

14 The source of this sonnet is Ronsard's 'Hier soir, Marie, en prenant maugré toy'.

16.1 and 2 'The Lesbian lad . . . gled your ging'. The 'lesbian lad' is Bacchus; Ceres is goddess of agriculture; Cylenus was tutor of Bacchus.

16.3 'Be blyth Kilburnie with the bairns of Beath'. Kilbirnie and Beith are in Ayrshire.

16.4 'And let Lochwinnoch'. Lochwinnoch is in Renfrewshire.

16.7 'swete Semple'. Lord Robert Semple, a noted Catholic and friend of Montgomerie.

16.12 'drunken Pancrage'. Presumably refers to another of the poet's cronies.

16.14 'Ih wachts, hale beir, fan hairts and nychsum drist'. Cranstoun in his Scottish Text Society edition admits that he can make little sense of this line. Almost certainly this is because Montgomerie is imitating the babblings of a drunken man. The general sense seems to be: 'Plenty of drink, good beer, fond hearts and a colossal thirst.'

17 Cf. Wyatt's 'They fle from me that sometyme did me seke', especially stanza 2.

17.5-8 'Art ye . . . me molest'. Ironic comment on the conventions of courtly love. He protests that love never permits him to sleep, while actually dreaming.

William Fowler
Texts: Nos. 18-21, *Drummond MS* (De 3.68); No. 22, *Hawthornden MS XI*

18 The source of this sonnet is Petrarch's 'Or che'l ciel e la terra e 'l vento tace', although ultimately it derives from Statius, 'Crimine quo merui . . .' It is the twenty-second sonnet in Fowler's sequence *The Tarantula of Love*.

18.14 'The fruits quhairoff are duble greiff, grones and smart'. Meikle in the Scottish Text Society edition reads 'doole', a word which Fowler often couples with 'greiff', but the MS reads 'duble'.

19 This is the forty-first sonnet in the *Tarantula*. It marks the poet's first brief escape from the tyranny of love.

19.12 'On grene'. Mediaeval colour symbolism represented green as the colour for hope and rebirth.

20 The forty-second sonnet in the *Tarantula*; it may well be the complaint to Nature mentioned in No. 41. The source is probably Sannazaro's sonnet 'O vita, vita non ma vivo affanno', although Hieronimo's famous lament in Kyd's *The Spanish Tragedy*, Act 3, is in the same tradition.
20.3 'Transchangd'. MS 'transchandge'.
21 The sixtieth sonnet in the *Tarantula*. After his short period of escape, the poet's lady, Bellisa, has resumed her tyranny. Two Petrarchan sonnets may have influenced this work, 'Son animali al mondo de sì altera' and 'Come talora al caldo tempo sòle'.
22 The seventh sonnet in the minor Hawthornden sequence. It is one of a group celebrating a stay the poet made in Orkney. The scribe has written in 'orknay' by way of explanation in the right hand margin.

Sir William Alexander
Text: *Aurora*, 1604

23 Cf. Petrarch, 'Amor mi sprona in un tempo et affrena'.
23.3 'Cadmus earth-borne troupes at jarres'. Cadmus created his troops by sowing the teeth of a dragon in the earth. On growing from the soil, they began to slay one another. Ovid, *Metamorphoses*, III, i ff.
23.12 'And in a moment make me glad and sad'. This is the sixth sonnet in Alexander's sequence, *Aurora*. The first nineteen sonnets explore the various paradoxes of the passion.
24.2 'That th'old philosophers were all but fooles'. His rejection of these philosophers is particularly meaningful, as he has relied heavily on Plato for ideas and images throughout the sequence.
25.1 and 2 'Oft have . . . be extreame'. The reference is to the theory of temperance advanced by James VI in many of his writings. Alexander, in disagreeing, continues the poetic sniping begun by the king in 'The complainte of the Muses to Alexander'.
26.1 'Awake my muse and leave to dreame of loves'. This is the last sonnet in *Aurora*. It leads on to a song celebrating marriage.
26.5 'with Joves stately bird'. The eagle.
26.9 and 10 'Ile tune . . . another field'. Cf. Spenser's avowed intention in *Amoretti* 80 of returning to composition of *The Faerie Queene*. Alexander is probably referring to his first play, *Darius*, which was composed after *Aurora* although appearing in print before it.

Sir David Murray
Text: *The Tragicall Death of Sophonisba*, 1611

29.2 'Behold heere Bellizarius'. Bellizarius, Lieutenant to the Emperor Justinian, was cruelly cast aside after he had outserved his usefulness. Murray, who was unwelcome at the English court after the death of his master, Prince Henry, may see a parallel in his own situation.

Notes

Alexander Craig
Text: *The Amorose Songes, Sonets, and Elegies*, 1606

30 Craig's sonnets are addressed to a variety of women, representing different aspects of love. This is one of those to 'Pandora' or Agnes Hay, later the wife of James, sixth Earl of Glencairn.

30.10 'Phosphor'. Phosphorus, the morning star.

30.12 'the fates alternall'. Orig. 'Fat's'. Craig often coins words suggesting two meanings. 'Alternall' has associations with both 'alternate' and 'eternal'.

31 Addressed to 'Penelope' or Penelope Rich, daughter of the first Earl of Essex and Sidney's 'Stella'. The original tale of 'the Persian king' is in Herodotus' *History*, Book 8, Chapter 118.

32 One of the sonnets addressed to Lais. In these poems Craig faces up to the problems of sexual infatuation.

33.1 'When Alexander did subdue and bring'. See Plutarch, *Life of Alexander*. The sonnet is again to Penelope.

34 The final sonnet in *The Amorose Songes*, addressed to Idea, who represents the highest, Platonic form of love.

34.3 and 4 'Thou, they and I . . . can not bee'. This relationship of poet to lady to verse is presented in terms associated with the Trinity. In view of Idea's spiritual power, this may well be an effect intended by the poet.

34.10 'fates'. Orig. 'fats'.

Sir Robert Ayton
Texts: No. 35, *Laing MS III, 436*; Nos. 36-9, *British Museum Additional MS 10308*.

36.1 'unto'. Ed. MS reads 'into'.

36.2 'art'. Ed. MS reads 'are'.

36.9 and 10 'But since . . . shaft of lead'. Cupid's golden darts caused love and his leaden ones repulsion.

37.1 'veiw'. This form was quite common in the late sixteenth and early seventeenth century.

The technique of facing a hypothetical refusal from the lady in successive quatrains and thus retreating into near despair was a favourite technique of Ayton's. It gave him that clear, logical base on which his wit functioned best.

38.1 'Faire famous flood'. The River Tweed.

38.2 'conjoynes two diadems in one'. The reference is to the Union of the Crowns in 1603.

38.6 'our captaines last farewell'. James VI crossing the Tweed to become King of England. Ayton asks the river not only to send the news out to the sea and, therefore, the wider world but also (l. 13) to carry it upstream to Melrose Abbey, where lies the heart of Scotland's great liberator in the Wars of Independence, Robert the Bruce.

38.11 'these'. Add. MS 28622. Add. MS 10308 reads 'this'.

38.12 'soon'. Add. MS 28622. Add. MS 10308 reads 'soe'.

39 A translation of Saint Amant's 'Assis sur un fagot, une pipe à la main'. See L. Kastner, 'Saint Amant and the English Poets', *Modern Language Review*, XXVI, 180-2.

39.5 'smyling'. Add. MS 28622. Add. MS 10308 reads 'simple'.

39.11 'make I'. Both MSS omit 'I'. It is metrically necessary and Sir John Ayton has made the required emendation in Add. MS 10308.

William Drummond

Texts: Nos. 40-3, *Poems* (Edinburgh), 1616; Nos. 44-6, *Flowres of Sion* (Edinburgh), 1630

40 The opening quatrain is based on Jean Passerat's 'Je sçay bien qu'icy bas rien ferme ne demeure'.

40.1 'all beneath the moone decayes'. All earthly things are transient. Luna herself symbolised change.

41 The source is Marino's 'O del Silenzio figlio, e della Notte'.

41.14 'I long to kisse the image of my death'. Drummond also uses the idea of sleep as an image of death in his major prose work, *A Cypresse Grove*.

42 Cf. William Fowler's sonnet, 'Fairweill, fair sant, may not the seas nor winds' (see *The Works of William Fowler*, ed. H. W. Meikle, Scottish Text Society, 3 vols. (Edinburgh and London, 1914-40), I, 251).

43 The octet is based on Tasso's 'Come in turbato ciel lucida stella'. The sestet comes from Tasso's 'Quasi celeste Diva, alzata à volo'.

43.7 'Till uglie Death'. The fear of death is a leitmotif in Drummond's writings. It dominates *Poems: the Second Part*, *A Cypresse Grove* and *Teares on the Death of Moeliades*. Only at the end of *Flowres of Sion* does he really come to terms with it.

45 Suggested by Desportes' sonnet, 'De foy, d'espoir, d'amour et de douleur comblée'.

45.13 'the Bethanian faire'. Mary Magdalene.

46 Drummond's theological problems, for ever in the background of his love poetry, dominate *Flowres of Sion*. In this sonnet he tries to reconcile the paradox of the world's worthlessness and God's beneficence; to accept humanity's limitations and face the fact of death.

Sir William Mure

Texts: No. 47, *The True Crucifixe for True Catholickes*, 1629; No. 48, *The Joy of Tears*, 1635

47.7 'Sinnes menstruous rags' – Isaiah, 30, verse 22. 'transparent laune' – Revelation 15, verse 6.

48 Mure, a dedicated covenanter, here makes an impassioned appeal on behalf of the church in Scotland, which he believes to be threatened by the 'heretical' ideas of Charles I. See R. D. S. Jack, 'Sir William Mure and the Covenant', *Records of the Scottish Church History Society*, XVIII, 2-6.

48.11 'The mouth of godly Zephanie is bard' – i.e. the voice of the prophets is ignored. Later in *The Joy of Tears* we learn that Amos and Jeremiah are also unheard.

Hugh Barclay

Text: *Drummond MS*

49.1 'My best belovit brother of the craft'. Alexander Montgomerie. Both poets suffered for their Catholic beliefs and Barclay was actually killed, when the Ailsa Craig conspiracy was discovered. See J. Paterson, *History of Ayr and Wigton* (Edinburgh, 1866), III, 296.

49.13 'opprest with barmie juggis' – i.e. with the thought of the drink he is missing.

Mark Alexander Boyd

Text: *Proof-pull, National Library of Scotland*

50 This is the most widely known of all Scottish sonnets. Its author, Mark Alexander Boyd, usually wrote in Latin.

50.5 'Twa gods gyds me' – i.e. Cupid and Venus.

50.10 'That teils the sand and sawis in the aire'. The reference is, of course, to futile occupations, but the phraseology suggests both the parable of the foolish builder and that of the sower.

INDEX OF AUTHORS

INDEX OF FIRST LINES